You May Kiss the Bride!

(Now What?)

The Essential Plan for the Marriage of Your Dreams

Happiness

Love

Faithfulness

Reginald A. Wickham

New York

You May Kiss the Bride! *(Now What?)*

By Reginald A. Wickham

© 2008 All rights reserved.

ISBN: 978-1-60037-338-1 (Paperback)
ISBN: 978-1-60037-339-8 (Hardcover)

Published by:

www.morganjamespublishing.com

Morgan James Publishing, LLC
1225 Franklin Ave. Suite 325
Garden City, NY 11530-1693
800.485.4943
www.MorganJamesPublishing.com

Cover & Interior Design by:

Megan Johnson
Johnson2Design
www.Johnson2Design.com
megan@Johnson2Design.com

Special thanks to…

My wife, Trudy Bell-Wickham, for her unwavering love and support. I love you so much! I always thought and believed "dream marriages" were possible. Now, thanks to you and our relationship, we have indeed achieved "the marriage of our dreams."

My parents, Eleanor M. Wickham and Reginald Wickham, who gave me the best possible example of a loving marriage. Congratulations on your 50th anniversary!

Elena Keegan, my personal coach who helped me develop the discipline required to take my idea from a concept and a deep passion to a manuscript and ultimately, this book.

Jody Ortiz, my literary coach and mentor. Thanks for your help, wisdom, advice, references, etc. This book would not have been the same without you.

Nancy Park for your wonderful drawings. Your artwork gave my book an extra breath of life.

The entire Morgan James Publishing staff, especially David Hancock, Ben Hancock, Carolyn Hancock and Margo Toulouse. Thank you for your belief in me and your dedication to my project, your vision and your expertise.

There are so many others who I'd like to thank for offering me support in various ways along this journey, including Renee Bacher and Claire Bateman for your wisdom, experience and candid thoughts and conversations regarding all aspects of writing. Also thanks to "The Gift of Goals" developed and/or facilitated by Jan Bernard, Elena Keegan, Babette Bourgeois and Trudy Bell-Wickham. Also thanks to my sister, Theresa M. Smith and to my friend, Anne Machonis.

Lastly, special thanks to "Mr. Reynolds" (Trudy's dog, my "step dog!") Thank you for keeping me company, lying by my side all hours of the night, weekends and basically anytime I could squeeze in time to write.

www.kissthebridenowwhat.com

Testimonials

*I*n case you are wondering why anyone would start a new life being in an "avoidable" debt, you should read this book! Yet it happens almost all the time. The debt comes from a wedding that is too expensive for the average couple. The average cost of a wedding is $40,000.00. How many people have that kind of money to spend and yet have nothing to show for it? Two days after the wedding all will see the ring and know that you are married, no matter how much the wedding cost you. No one would know how much debt you incurred except you, a debt that may take years to eliminate. Would it not be nice to use that money for a down payment on a home?

In the light of the exaggerated emphasis on wedding – which is nothing but a thirty to forty-five minute ceremony followed by three to four hours of partying – it is refreshing to have someone who is calling us to shift our emphasis from **wedding** to **marriage** – which is a life long commitment and relationship.

This book does a wonderful job of not telling you *what decision to make* but gives you a wealth of information. It tells you the important things to consider and what your options are so as to enable you to make a wise and practical decision. "It is my sincere hope that within the pages of this book you'll discover ... before any vows are exchanged ... that the one you're uniting with will be your partner for life."

  – Rev. Joseph Awotwi, M.D., *is currently the pastor of Saint Mark United Methodist Church in Baton Rouge, Louisiana. He is a Board Certified Pediatrician who had a private Pediatric practice for many years in New Orleans. He received his M.Div from Duke Divinity School and is presently working on his certification as Spiritual Director and Retreat Leader.*

In "You May Kiss The Bride," Reginald Wickham offers "common sense keys" to open up lines of communication, and to explore the sensitive concerns of newlyweds. Marriage planning, in this book, becomes an open invitation to discuss both the major and minor issues of a lifetime relationship.

Couples will capture a vision of their future together, through open dialogue and compromise about many of the challenges described in this smorgasbord of marital options. In doing so, the reader will experience a taste of "Wickham wisdom."

Even better, the author unties many relationship snarls for those who are really serious about "tying the knot."

Dr. Gwendolyn Goldsby Grant, *multi-media psychologist, contributing relationship expert ESSENCE MAGAZINE, and author of* The Best Kind of Loving.

What an awesome comprehensive collection of information for those planning a wedding and/or those currently married. This is a working tool written by someone who obviously understands the basic tools and principles of establishing an effective relationship. Mr. Wickham has produced a very impressive work.

Rev. Dr. LILLIE S. CANNON, *associate minister of Cumberland Free Will Baptist Church, financial counselor, motivation speaker, author, and entrepreneur Lillie S. Cannon, PhD*

You May Kiss the Bride! (Now what?) The Essential Plan for the Marriage of Your Dreams! is an easy to read guide for couples looking for good basic information on how to live together after the big day is a just a memory, whether newly engaged or newly married. As a financial professional working with couples and individuals to help them achieve financial goals, I was pleased to see practical advice around sharing experiences and expectations about money.

Wende Padek, *Financial Advisor*

Table of Contents

Introduction

Marriage – The art of blending or merging two separate lives into one unit, one entity – a new family.

– Reginald Wickham

This book was not written with the intention of telling a newlywed couple what they must do in order to have a successful marriage. It's not instructional in that sense.

Instead, this book highlights many areas and topics that should be discussed before getting married and throughout the duration of your marriage – especially in the earlier years while you're still negotiating your life together as a married couple.

I believe in the hoopla of being engaged and planning for your wedding; many times these topics remain unthought-of. And if they are thought-of, they go unspoken. They are not at all communicated. Or perhaps worse, they are assumed. Because of this, each of you getting married may have your own preconceived notions. If you and your partner's preconceived notions don't match, that's where problems may arise.

Neither of you are necessarily "right" nor "wrong," but both of you won't be happy or satisfied in that specific area until it is resolved.

Love is also an important element in a marriage. Some may argue that it's the most important element. However, it's not the only element in a good, solid marriage. I have no doubt you will provide the love you'll need. Hopefully, this book will provide a common sense roadmap designed to open dialogue between both of you and help you understand any major and minor issues that may surface at various times during your marriage.

The purpose of this book is to identify where there are discrepancies in how you and your partner look at particular areas regarding your relationship and living together as a married couple. Once the areas are identified, you can be creative in finding solutions to ensure that both of you are fulfilled and your individual needs and the needs of your relationship are satisfied – hopefully before it mushrooms or blows up into a major issue.

All the information in this book is of a general nature and is furnished for educational purposes only. No information contained in this book is to be taken as legal, financial or any other type of advice pertaining to any individual's specific premarital or marital needs. The information is not a recommendation for a particular course of action regarding your financial, legal or any other matters and is not intended to provide specific advice.

The Wickford Group and their creators, advisors, consultants, editors, wholesalers, distributors and retailers are not liable or responsible, in whole or in part, to any person or entity for any injury, damage, or loss of any sort caused or alleged to be caused directly or indirectly by the use, practice, teaching, or other dissemination of any of the techniques, information, or ideas presented in this book.

It remains your responsibility to evaluate the accuracy, completeness, and usefulness of all information provided by the Wickford Group.

Chapter One

Why I Wrote This Book

Love at first sight is easy to understand; it's when two people have been looking at each other for a lifetime that it becomes a miracle.

– Amy Bloom

*H*ow it all started…

My wife and I are an older couple and have been married a little over a year. This is a second marriage for both of us. We jokingly say that we both married the wrong person many years ago. (But that's okay; they may very well be saying the same thing about us!) Destiny, in the form of a mutual friend, introduced us to one another as we enjoyed a trip to the horse races with friends (a camouflaged blind-date) a couple of years ago.

It wasn't exactly love a first sight. It was more like "Wow! That's a nice, intelligent person to talk to and hang out with" at first sight. Nonetheless, as lady luck would have it, we began to date, which soon led to an engagement.

Our engagement was a short one, only six months long. Most people told us, "That's not enough time to plan for a wedding." Or, "You two are crazy if you think you can pull off planning a wedding in only six months!"

Although some of our friends and family members had their doubts, we knew we had plenty of time to plan the right kind of wedding for us. We're both mature and resourceful; besides, I was the type of groom-to-be who was more than willing and also capable of assisting my fiancée with the wedding and reception plans.

It was because of my willingness to participate and support my fiancée in any way possible, that I agreed to attend a "Bridal Show." And, it was on this day that I realized I would merely be a co-star, or supporting actor, at best, on our wedding day. My bride-to-be was going to be the one and only star of the show!

When we arrived at the "Bridal Show," I felt the excitement all around me. It was as if the entire place had wedding fever. But before we could join in the excitement, we had to register. The hosts warmly greeted my fiancée, checked out **her** engagement ring giving **her** a "thumbs up," congratulated **her** on **her** upcoming wedding and handed **her** a registration form and a clipboard. They didn't even acknowledge me or look in my direction. I felt as though I was invisible. This was to be my first taste of reality. This was when I began to realize my true role in this process.

I watched over my fiancée's shoulder as she filled out the registration form, providing them with plenty of information. The form asked for **her** name, address, home phone number, work phone number, fax number, cell phone number, wedding date, number of people in the wedding party, wedding location, if known, honeymoon location, if known, etc.

When she completed the form, it dawned on me…there wasn't even a place for her to fill in the groom's name, much less any other information about me. Again, I felt as though I was invisible and certainly not a participant in the event. But, hold on to your seats! I was to become very visible at the next station.

The next desk we were whisked to was – you guessed it – the admissions booth. When we had to pay admission to the "Bridal Show," I was suddenly recognized. The woman behind the admissions booth quoted the price and stuck her hand out in **my** direction, waiting for payment.

After I paid **our** admission, you wouldn't believe what happened. The woman, who had just collected the admission fee from me, gave my fiancée a name tag and a shopping bag full of gifts, brochures and other information and goodies.

You know, I could kick myself sometimes for asking stupid questions, but I asked this one before thinking…"Err, excuse me Ma'am, but I didn't get my name tag. May I have one?" Dumb, dumb, dumb…

She looked at me, her eyes piercing a hole deep into my heart, "*You* don't get a name tag. Only our *brides* get a name tag!"

My fiancée probably didn't know how I was feeling because she just giggled with delight! I did my best to smile, although I felt small and humiliated. I struggled to suppress my disdain for the entire process, knowing that we'd only just begun.

I thought…*No wonder most guys don't like coming to these things*.

We entered the "Bridal Show" and the first booth we came to, ironically, represented a tuxedo store.

I was internally thrilled! *Now I'll get some recognition*, I thought to myself! *Now I'll get some respect!* The gentleman behind the booth came around to the front in anticipation of greeting us. He stuck out his hand and greeted my fiancée. *Drat! Foiled again!* But, he did greet me afterwards. Maybe it was the expression on my face? Maybe not!

Anyway, he asked many of the same questions that my fiancée filled out in the registration letter. At least this time he did ask for my name. The tuxedo store representative gleefully shared that we could qualify for a free tuxedo rental for the groom. *That would be me! It was the first time I was the one who was going to receive something!* He also told us that we could even qualify for a free honeymoon. *Uh oh…what's the catch?* He asked us how many people were in our wedding party; how many tuxedos would we be renting. I shrugged my shoulders, "Two. Maybe three."

He obviously didn't like my answer, because he immediately turned away from me and asked my fiancée the very same question. "How many tuxedos do you plan on renting?" She answered, "Hopefully three." *Hello! I'm the groom! It's my groomsmen who will be wearing the tuxedos!*

The tuxedo guy asked us one more time, very slowly, deliberately and much louder as though we were having a difficult time understanding English… "How many tuxes will you need? 5? 10? 15? If you rent seven, you'll get the groom's tuxedo for free! If you rent 10, then you get a free limo. If you rent 15, then you'll qualify for a free honeymoon to one of six destinations."

So I answered him just as slowly, deliberately and perhaps a little louder using two and three fingers respectively as visual aids, explaining once again that we'd only need a couple of tuxes. When he finally understood that our wedding was going to be very small and, specifically, our wedding party was going to consist of a bride, groom, two bridesmaids and two groomsmen, he basically dropped us like a hot potato.

On to the next booth…

We were moved like cattle from booth to booth because the place was filling up, and there were so many brides and their mothers along with a few brave grooms to accommodate.

Our next stop was the bridal gown booth. Here, my fiancée was asked what kind of gown she was looking for. She, thankfully, is very reasonable and resourceful. She'd already decided that she didn't want a traditional, lavish wedding gown, especially since this is her second marriage, and instead opted for a non-traditional gown.

She explained that she wanted a very classy, elegant gown or perhaps even a dress, and that she didn't feel she had to pay an arm and a leg for it. They tried their very best to convince her that this is a once in a lifetime day and, "wouldn't it be a shame when you're reviewing your wedding pictures that you see yourself dressed in something less than what you really want and deserve?"

We frowned as we watched the models in wedding gowns walk down the elevated runway, strutting their stuff, back and forth, struggling to continue smiling for what must have seemed like hours. They were underneath the hot, hot spotlights, dressed in uncomfortable gowns while photographers snapped scores of rapid-fire exposures. I smiled to myself. All I could think of was how the models reminded me of French fries being kept hot under a heat lamp at a fast food restaurant.

Again, when the wedding gown folks finally understood the fact that we were planning a small, simple wedding, they abruptly looked past us to welcome the next in line. *Hmmmm, I noticed a pattern developing…*

We negotiated through the rest of the "Bridal Show." Most folks who manned the booths jumped out of their seat to greet my fiancée, introducing themselves and their services, showing her pictures, samples and distributing their cards, pamphlets, etc. without uttering a word to me or acknowledging that I even existed. I continued to feel as though I was invisible, but I was resolved to let it rest and got used to it.

We stopped by booths representing:

* Reception halls – the number of guests they catered to was either 100 or 150 and up. (We only planned to invite 50 – 60 of our closest friends and family. *Bah, humbug!*)
* Several catering booths – some of them had samples of their goodies. I was astounded at how many of them featured chocolate fountains with strawberries for dipping. That must have been the "in" thing that year.
* Photographers

- DJs – we actually planned to have a real band at our small but elegant wedding reception. *Gee, that didn't go over very well at the DJ booth!*

- Wedding cake confectioners – we actually hired one of the vendors we met at the show!

- Videographers

- Limousine companies

- Florists

- Stationers – for invitations, announcements, napkins, wedding programs, thank you cards, etc.

- Travel agents – specializing in honeymoon destinations and cruises

- Jewelers

- Bridal/Wedding consultants – like conductors of a symphony orchestra making all of the individual parts perform beautifully as a whole

- Stores carrying accessories for the bride including hosiery, head pieces, veils, shoes, etc.

- Make up artists, facials, manicures, pedicures, massages, etc.

After we visited every single booth at the show we were exhausted. We didn't even stick around for the "free" prizes and drawings. We simply wanted to get out of there.

Honestly, the "Bridal Show" we attended offered a plethora of good information, all in one place. Perfect - if you have an idea of what you're looking for. Overwhelming - if you're just starting to plan a wedding - looking for ideas.

I felt kind of sad as I was leaving; not for us, but for the hundreds of young brides/couples and parents of the brides who have to make so many choices just for one day of their married lives together.

I feel horrible that so much planning is put into a four hour party. (When I distill it and break it down to its lowest level, that's my description of a wedding reception – a lovely, memorable, four-hour party.) And, relatively speaking, very little planning is put into the rest of the marriage.

I've been told that my distilled description of a wedding reception, "a four hour party," is too harsh. If you agree that it's too harsh, then what about these descriptions? "A festive gala. The social event of a lifetime! A beautiful, day long celebration marking the beginning of your new life together!" Take your pick or use your own definition but please, let's not get lost in semantics.

I told my fiancée, "I certainly hope we put as much effort into ventures of our choosing after we're married!" The amount of time, energy, and effort that goes into wedding planning, if applied elsewhere, could be analogous to planning for a business start-up or creating an invention or developing the cure for a disease that could lead to a better society, not to mention a lifetime of financial independence!

Don't get me wrong, celebrating is good! Celebrations are great! A wedding is a life event that should be celebrated!

I know this may not be in line with conventional thoughts and feelings, but I believe there should be at least as much time, effort and energy spent concentrating on the *marriage* as is spent on the wedding and reception. No wonder the folks manning the booths didn't come running to greet me!

I thought…If I sponsored a "Bridal Show" – first of all, it wouldn't be called a "Bridal Show." It would be called a "Marriage Show," or better yet, a "Life Show," and I'd invite entities like:

* Marriage/Relationship Counselors,
* Financial/Investment Planners,
* Legal Advisors,
* Home Decorating Consultants,
* Planned Parenthood,
* Health & Fitness Counselors,
* Medical Professionals,
* Nutritionists,
* Spiritual Health Leaders,
* Cooking Instructors,

- Apartment Rental Agents,

- Real Estate Agents,

- Mortgage Agents,

- Insurance Agents,

- Career/Employment Consultants,

- Retirement Specialists,

- Home Depot, Lowe's, etc…

So you see my idea of a "Life Show" would be about the business of managing a marriage – after the wedding and reception are over and after returning from your honeymoon. (Sadly, I believed that it probably wouldn't be as well-attended as a Bridal Show, either!)

I shared this idea with an audience who attended a speech I was giving. My audience was composed of a group of co-workers - professional people in a speech making club. To my surprise, many of them said that they wish they could have attended a "Life Show" before they got married. Or, they wish their son/daughter could have attended a "Life Show" before they got married. Or, they know someone about to get married and wouldn't it be great if they could attend a "Life Show!"

Hmmmm… Maybe my "Life Show" would be well attended after all. And, maybe I should write down all of my ideas and thoughts…

Well there you have it…An idea was born!

Most Engaged Couples Never Look Past the Big Day

If ever two were one, then surely we.
If ever man were loved by wife, then thee.

– Anne Bradstreet

*W*e all know that weddings are big business in our country. This fact is clearly illustrated not only by the bridal shows, but also by the $125 billion dollars spent each year in the wedding industry on things such as venues, dresses, tuxes, limos, cakes, flowers, receptions, pictures, etc.

In 2005, the Fairchild Bridal Group conducted a survey of over 1,000 brides. They discovered the average amount paid out for a wedding was almost $30,000.[1] That's $30,000 for a one day event; a "four hour party!"

This figure would be understandable to me if the divorce rate in this country was not at an all-time high. That's the sad part, because instead of spending that amount of money on a wedding, some couples would be better off investing in college or saving for a down payment on a home.

Don't get me wrong! I'm not suggesting that couples should skimp on their wedding or forego their wedding reception. That's not what this book is about, at all. I just wonder what would happen to the divorce rate in this country if couples focused as much attention on planning their next 2, 5, 10, 20, 40, or 50 years together as they do on things like their shower, wedding, reception and honeymoon.

I've known many couples, both young and old, who fell in love and announced their engagement to friends and family. Typically, the first question asked is "When's the date?" That question is soon followed with "Who will be in the bridal party?" Then, "Where will it be?" And finally, "Have you thought about where you want to go on your honeymoon?"

These questions are all natural to ask because when you find out a loved one is getting married, these are the first things that pop into your head.

However, if one is thinking about the long-term for the couple, he or she may ask questions such as "During you courtship have there been any red flags that you've seen and ignored? Do you have a plan to address and resolve them before you get married? Besides loving each other, enjoying great sex and having lots of fun together, have you given any thought to how your married life will be? Do you have similar or compatible goals in life?" or even "Of all of the relationships you've had, what makes this one so different or special that you want to get married?"

At the time of an engagement, couples are so caught up in emotions, excitement and expectations for the big day that they often don't see past the honeymoon. Then after the vows have been exchanged, the final toast raised, the last song played, the presents opened and after the lovely couple returns from their honeymoon, normal life sets in and it can be overwhelming. Couples find themselves lost and confused about whether or not they made the right choice for their life partner, because they're suddenly hit with life issues that they haven't discussed or thought about.

It's my sincere hope that within the pages of this book you'll discover a guide to create a marriage that will be built on a solid foundation, before any vows are exchanged, and you'll have total confidence that the one you're uniting with will be your partner for life.

Questions to Ask Before Taking the Leap

*A*t the end of each chapter in this book you'll find thought provoking questions that are related to the topic of the chapter to ask your fiancé and/or yourself.

1. Is your fiancé open to making a marriage plan before you say your "I do's?"

2. If you're newly married, what do you feel you overlooked when planning for your marriage that needs to be discussed at this point?

3. Do you and your fiancé/spouse relate well with one another?

4. Do you and your partner understand and utilize good communication skills?

5. Can you talk to your fiancé/spouse about anything/everything?

6. Is there anything that you've always wanted to share with your fiancé/spouse that you've been avoiding until now?

7. Is there anything relevant to your marriage that you want or need to know about your fiancé/spouse that you've been afraid to ask?

8. Have you and your fiancé/spouse taken any communication courses or seminars?

9. Do you feel that your communication skills are compatible?

10. Do you think a refresher course would be valuable?

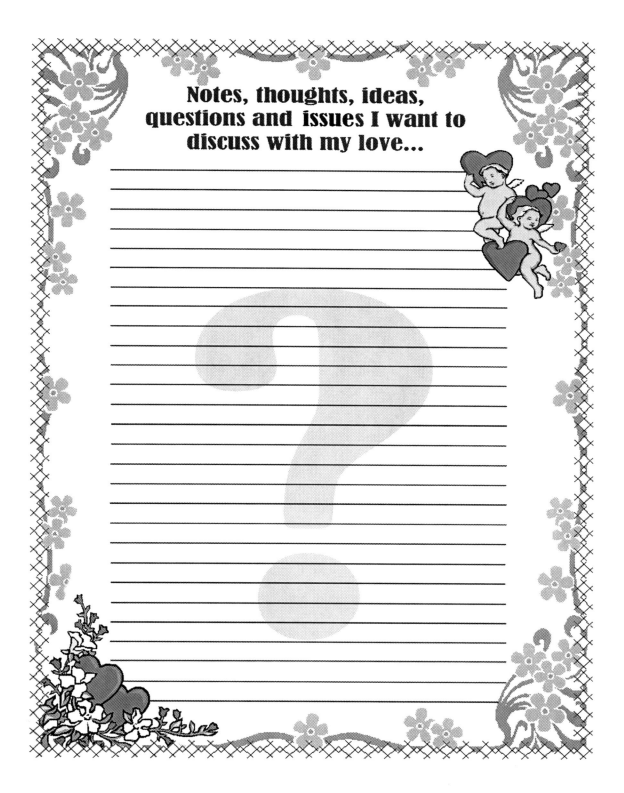

Notes, thoughts, ideas, questions and issues I want to discuss with my love...

Chapter Two
Pre-Marital Legal Matters

For two people in a marriage to live together day after day is unquestionably the one miracle the Vatican has overlooked.

– Bill Cosby

*L*egal matters can be a touchy subject for anyone to discuss, especially couples who are at the point in their relationship when they're deciding if it's time to move forward and make a commitment.

The last thing you want to do is spoil the romance by bringing up topics such as prenuptial agreements, background checks, or living wills before you pop the question or answer "Yes!" to the question. These topics are taboo, and usually aren't brought up until long after the wedding date is set, if they're ever discussed at all.

This is most unfortunate, because it's these types of matters that should be worked out before any type of commitment is made. Think about it. What if you've dated someone for a couple of years and *then* found out they have a poor credit rating, after you've announced to all your friends and family the "happy" news that you're engaged. What now? Would you then ditch them because they're irresponsible? Would you worry that if they ruined their own credit, they could do the same to yours? Would you go through with the engagement, wedding and marriage or begin searching for a way out of the relationship?

Just think of the headache you would save yourself if you discovered who you're dating before you decide to commit.

I once knew a gentleman who was a decent, hard working guy. He held down a steady nine to five job in a professional office, and was a self-proclaimed bachelor. He was a big guy, and wasn't really "all that" with the ladies. Well, you can imagine the happiness his friends and family felt for him when he announced one day that he'd found the love of his life and was getting hitched! All of us, his friends, family and co-workers, were truly excited for him and wished him the best of luck.

Joy soon turned to sorrow as the newlywed man who had been married for less than a month announced that he was getting a divorce. You can imagine the shock, surprise, and horror that everyone felt for him!

We automatically assumed the fault had to be hers, because he was such a nice, caring guy. We couldn't imagine a woman who had loved him enough to marry him would leave him so soon. But we were wrong!

Apparently, the man had racked up quite a lot of debt and spent most of his adult life enjoying being on his own and living footloose and carefree. He didn't pay much heed to things like bills, due dates or credit. And the woman who married him had no clue.

As soon as the honeymoon was over, he confessed to his new bride that if he needed credit to breathe, he'd suffocate and die. It was hard to believe that he would wait until after the wedding to confide in her, but he did.

She didn't take the news very well. She packed up her things and moved back to her place, while thanking her lucky stars that she hadn't sold it yet.

I'm not telling this story to bring you down or make you doubt that you'll have a future with your intended if you've been remiss with your own credit. And I'm not suggesting that if and when you find out that your mate's credit history is not pristine the only remedy is to dump them. I'm telling this story to drive home the very important, much too often overlooked point that you must look deep inside a person and find out who they are, what they want from life, where they've been and how much they're worth, financially, emotionally and morally, long before you plan to build a life with them.

Once you know who they are you can then make an *informed decision* about whether or not they are the one for you.

Background Checks

Any one must see at a glance that if men and women marry those whom they do not love, they must love those whom they do not marry.

– Harriet Martineau

> **Would you want a background check or a credit check performed on your spouse-to-be?**
>
> **Would you give a background check or a credit check on yourself to your spouse-to-be?**

Why on earth would anyone even consider having a credit check or any other kind of background check performed on the person they were about to marry? I've already given you one example of what can happen if you decide to forego this important step. But also consider the fact that their background becomes your background and vice versa once you marry. Your backgrounds become jointly attached the moment you say your "I do's."

Similarly, as soon as you become married, if either of you have had any financial judgments, they're automatically inherited by the other party, as well as anything else that may be in either of your financial pasts.

Let's say you had a civil judgment against you in a real estate transaction that went bad. A year or so down the road you get married, and you and your spouse had planned to purchase a house together. When you go to a financial institution to acquire a mortgage this judgment will come up, and depending on its severity, it could very well prevent both of you from getting the mortgage you needed to purchase your house, even if your spouse has a history of impeccable credit.

Doesn't your significant other have a right to know and understand what potential issues they may face if they marry you? On the other hand, what if it were your significant other who may have had a history of bad credit? Would you want to be aware of this fact up front? Or would you prefer to be surprised, shocked and stunned when you find out at a most inopportune time?

Maybe over dinner at one of your favorite restaurants you could say, "Hey honey, let's get his and hers credit checks!" Or maybe not!

This would indeed be a difficult subject to discuss. Many people may not understand your motivation for wanting a credit, or any other kind of background check performed on them. After all, "Don't you love me?" "If you loved me, you wouldn't even think of such a thing!"

As the song goes, "What's love got to do with it?" Wanting to understand your significant other's credit history doesn't conflict with your ability to love them. I mean, you love your intended, the person you're going to marry, right? Yet, you've asked them about their family history, their spiritual history, their educational history, their social history, their health, where they were born, grew up, their emotional history, etc. Most likely, you've probably even discussed, at least, some of their past relationships.

Background and/or credit checks are additional pieces of information that help you understand the person that you will wed and be connected to for the rest of your life. Having background and credit checks done on the behalf of both of you may be a good idea in general. Knowing what is included on your credit report is crucial. There are too many cases where incorrect data is linked to individuals on their credit reports. This, actually, is an opportune time to insure that your credit report is correct. But if you have any reason to believe your fiancé may be hiding something from the past, you'll especially want to know. Ultimately, their past can and will affect your future.

Let's say your fiancé always pays with cash, or they use their credit card daily and seem to spend more than they could possibly be earning, you may then be more motivated to clear this issue from your mind.

Think about it this way, before you're approved by government officials to foster or adopt a child, you must pass health requirements, financial requirements, legal requirements, age requirements and more to ensure that the chances are good that you're going to be a suitable candidate to raise the child. You have to pass criminal checks through state and/or federal agencies to prove that you don't have a criminal history or any history of child abuse. And, you're evaluated by a social worker to ensure that you have an idea of the proper way to parent, to show you can provide a proper home, and that you're mentally stable.

If you have to go through all of those things to bring a child into your home, shouldn't you give at least a fraction of this type of consideration for someone who will be spending many years laying by your side night after night and sharing in decisions about where your finances will be spent? Does this help to shed some light on the reason why you need to be sure of whom it is you're marrying?

Divorce is so common these days that people casually say things like, "We'll try out marriage and see if it works. If it doesn't work out, there is always divorce." Just imagine what the world would be like if everybody thought this way. Unfortunately, things seem to be heading in that direction -- fast. Many people would feel betrayed if they found out their partner misrep-

resented themselves. They feel that life is way too precious to spend one second in a marriage where they don't trust their partner. That's why learning everything you possibly can ahead of time is so important.

I realize that bringing up the topic of past credit history can be daunting. One way that can possibly take the sting out of introducing this subject to your fiancé is to take the initiative and present them with your credit history. Or, you can invite them to have a credit check performed on you. After all, what's good for the goose is good for the gander.

If your fiancé is violently opposed to your having a credit check performed on them, you'll have to determine what that means. Does it mean that they are opposed to credit checks performed on one another, in general? Or does it mean they have something to hide that they don't want exposed? Or should I say, they don't want it exposed now?

Whether they're ready to face it or not, it's likely that sooner or later it will expose itself. But by then, their history will be intimately intertwined with your own.

Prenuptials

A good marriage is at least 80 percent good luck in finding the right person at the right time. The rest is trust.

– Nanette Newman

This can potentially be one of the most volatile subjects you discuss on your journey to marriage. It can be a highly emotionally charged subject. Some people have opposing or differing opinions regarding the very idea of prenuptial agreements. It also can ignite heated debates and arguments based on different religious points of view and can cause your intended to feel as if you don't trust them or you don't have any hope that your marriage will last.

So, why would you ever want to consider a prenuptial agreement?

The words "'Til death do us part" are spoken every day in this country, but sadly, only half of the people who say this actually live up to it. Did you ever

have a boyfriend or girlfriend that you adored so much you thought you'd be together for the rest of your lives? We all have a relationship like that at one time or another, but unfortunately life sometimes gets in the way and it ends way too soon.

Therefore, if one partner has inherited money or has amassed a good deal of savings or material items, they are protected with a prenup from having the court divide up their pre-marital assets.

Consider spending years with a partner and then having to divide up not only the material items you've obtained, but also the financial investments, savings, stocks bonds, retirement plans, etc. that you have accumulated both during and before your marriage. Can you imagine the future headaches you could save by deciding who gets what now, instead of at a time when you're both emotionally drained and not in agreement on anything, much less the division of property?

The last thing you want to think about now is the untimely death of your upcoming marriage, but if you plan for the future, you'll have less stress, worry, and headache later.

First of all, what is a prenuptial agreement?

Prenuptial agreements are legal in every state in the United States. It's only legal; however, if it's in writing, has a full disclosure of all the legal assets of both parties before the marriage, and is signed by both the husband and wife.

It's a protection for both parties involved in the marriage in case of divorce by clearly stating the parties marital assets before the "I do's."

A common myth with prenuptial agreements is that they must be drawn up by an attorney to be a legal document. This is untrue. As long as the agreement meets all of the above factors, it's legal and can be upheld in court. Understand, though, that a spouse has the right to contest a prenuptial agreement, and it's up to the judge to decide if in fact all of the legal parameters have been met, so it's always best to consult an attorney before investing your livelihood in a document that could be found null and void.

Which couples would be good candidates for a prenuptial agreement?

Have you amassed significant assets or is there a significant difference in your assets versus your fiancé's?

Do you own a home?

Do you own a business?

Do you have children from a previous relationship?

Have you accumulated significant debt or is there a significant difference in your liabilities versus your fiancé's?

Prenuptials are commonly used by individuals who have children from a previous marriage and want to ensure in case of death and/or divorce that either some or the majority of their assets would go to their children instead of everything going to their current spouse. Prenuptials are also used by couples when one or both parties have significant assets or when there is a large difference between one party's assets or liabilities versus the other party.

Good candidates for this type of agreement usually include:

* Individuals with children from a prior marriage or relationship;
* Individuals with a large amount of cash, bonds, stocks, mutual funds, CDs, real estate or investments;
* Rental and commercial property owners;
* Individuals with higher levels of education that produce large amounts of income;
* Business owners;
* Individuals with a great amount of debt;
* Individuals with retirement plans, 401 K plans, and inheritances.

Which couples absolutely don't need a prenuptial agreement?

If you are both young, and you or your intended don't really have a significant amount of assets or debt and there are no children prior to your engagement, a prenuptial agreement may be a waste of time.

If you learn that your assets and the assets your fiancé has accumulated is equivalent, even though neither of you are opposed to the concept of a prenuptial agreement, you may still decide that you don't want or need a prenuptial agreement.

However, there are topics in a prenuptial agreement that could save you from arguments in the future, such as:

* Automobile ownership;
* Rights to transfer property;
* Terms in case of future divorce for spousal support;
* Distribution of marital assets in case of divorce;
* Distribution of assets in case of death;
* Distribution of life insurance policy in case of death;
* Guidelines for raising children – education, religion, discipline, values, rewards, etc.;

* Anything else that may affect the marriage.

If both of you agree, for what ever reasons, that you don't want or need a prenuptial agreement, then it's easy! Don't get one. End of story!

What happens if one of you wants a prenuptial agreement and the other does not want one?

Logically, in most cases when one partner wants a prenuptial agreement and the other does not, it's the partner who has considerably more assets who wants it and the partner who has fewer assets who doesn't. Or, the partner who has no debt may want to sign a prenuptial agreement and the partner who has amassed considerable debt may not want to sign.

The problem arises when one of you is in favor of having a prenuptial agreement and the other is opposed to signing one. Certainly it's possible, but this author has never heard of a case where the partner who has considerably less assets or considerably more debt is the one who insists on signing a prenuptial agreement. Similarly, I've never heard of a case in which the partner who has considerably more assets, (or less debt), is the one in the relationship who insists on not having/signing a prenuptial agreement.

So, let's take the statistically, more normal case – where the partner who has less assets does not want to sign a prenuptial agreement and the partner who has more assets wants to sign one.

The partner who wants to sign a prenuptial agreement may have some of the typical reasons for doing so. What is earned as a married couple should be shared and shared alike, but what has been worked for and accumulated prior to the marriage should remain independent of the household trust.

Once married, why should a partner instantly take a quantum leap forward in his or her net worth while the other takes a similar quantum leap backwards?

Example: Becky and Ken are getting married. Becky is worth $1,000,000 and Ken is in debt to the tune of $200,000. If they don't sign a prenuptial agreement, when they get married and say "I do," instantly Becky and Ken's net worth will be [$1,000,000 + (-$200,000) = $800,000].

Let's say in a period of three years they accumulate $100,000 as a married couple. Now their net worth is [$800,000 + 100,000 = $900,000] If, in the horrible event of a divorce, they were legally required to split their assets "50-50,"

Becky would be entitled to half of $900,000 and so would Ken, meaning they both would walk away from the marriage with $450,000 each.

Wait a minute! Becky was worth $1,000,000 before she married Ken and now after three years of marriage her net worth decreased by 55% to $450,000? During the same period of time, Ken was $200,000 in debt before tying the knot and now, after three years of marriage not only is he out of debt, he's now worth $450,000 too?

In this example, Becky's net worth decreased from $1,000,000 to $450,000 in three short years of marriage. And Ken went from owing $200,000 to being $450,000 in the black. Or put yet another way, Becky lost $550,000 from the day they said "I do" to the day their divorce was final while Ken actually gained $650,000 in the same amount of time.

After three years of marriage, Ken gained a considerable amount and Becky lost a considerable amount because there was no prenuptial agreement in place that stated the partner's assets before marriage and which partner would be entitled to what in case of a split. Some folks will see this example and simply say, "That's just the way marriage works." Others will see this example and schedule an appointment with their attorney before reading the next sentence!

Where does religion fall into play?

If you keep up with popular culture at all, you've probably heard that two very famous and popular personalities who were married split up partly because of a disagreement over whether or not to raise their children in the Catholic Church (the religion of one of them) or the Scientologist Church (the religion that the other converted to during the marriage). Whether or not this is true, I don't know. But I do know that arguments over how to raise children in families where spouses have different religions, or where one spouse converts to a different religion, can be a factor leading to divorce.

Prenuptial agreements can be worded in a way that clearly states that if children born as a result of the union, the children will be raised a certain way. This agreement not only helps to minimize the amount of religious-based arguments, it also gives both of the partners' guidelines to follow in raising their children in general.

If one or both of the partners convert to a religion other than the one agreed upon during the time of marriage, and both partners agree to raise the children in the new religion, a new agreement can be drawn up stating that the section of the prenuptials in which religion was agreed upon is null and void.

What about the argument – Getting a prenuptial agreement is just preparing for a divorce?

Some say that signing a prenuptial agreement is like planning for divorce. Marriage is very much a merging of two entities, just as when two corporate entities merge. The corporations don't merge thinking they're going to split up, but you can be sure that each of their financial statements have been meticulously prepared by the best of accounting firms, and lawyers from each company contribute to drawing up the soundest legal documents; protecting the interests of all parties concerned.

So, does that mean that when two corporations merge, just because they have planned ahead legally and financially, they'll eventually split? Hardly! Having a contingency plan in place is merely a form of self-protection. It's just smart planning.

What about the argument… if anything were to happen to our marriage, I would be fair. I wouldn't try to take all of your money.

(Yeah, right!) I mean, the person saying that could very well mean every bit of it while they're saying it. But, in an emotionally charged divorce, who knows what they might say?

A response to that would be…if you'd be fair and equitable during a divorce, why not simply sign this prenuptial agreement stating the same?

If your prenuptial isn't all about financial or material topics, but includes things such as religion, child-rearing, planning for you or your spouses parents as they age, etc. your partner may possibly be more open to the idea of planning ahead.

Will our prenuptial agreement expire after a few years of marriage?

You may agree that after you've been married for a pre-specified amount of time your prenuptial agreement can be retired. If ever both of you agree that the prenup has lost its usefulness, you can agree to deem it null and void.

A prenup, if you choose, can have an expiration date. It's up to you.

So how do I bring up the idea of creating a prenuptial?

This subject matter should be approached in a careful, respectful, courteous, and honest manner. When do you bring up the dreaded subject? There may never be a great time, but if you're considering getting one, the earlier the better.

If your relationship is serious, you're both committed to one another, and you've discussed marriage – the topic of a prenuptial agreement can be discussed. Some couples talk about a prenuptial agreement before they are even engaged.

The worst thing to do if you're considering a prenup is to wait too long. Many states require that a prenup be signed by both parties well in advance of the wedding. This is to protect both parties from feeling forced to sign the prenup or signing it as a result of pressure, an ultimatum or in a state of duress.

Be sure you understand why you want the agreement. Your fiancé will certainly want to understand your reason(s). Also, be sure to be perfectly honest, candid, and open regarding this subject – and every other subject between you and your intended, for that matter.

Although the math is correct, the figures used in the prenup example are admittedly inflated. Most of us do not have assets or debts this large. How about a more realistic example…

Debbie and Bruce got married on the same day and got divorced within a month of Becky and Ken. On the day they got married, Debbie was worth $10,000. (She worked and diligently saved a couple of grand each year for five years.) Bruce was in debt by $2,000. (He amassed a savings of $2,500 but he still owed $4,500 in school loans.) Let's say in the three years they were married they managed to put aside $3,000 but they still owed $2,000 on the new furniture they purchased – so their net gain was $1,000.

In this example after three years of marriage Debbie's and Bruce's combined net worth is [$10,000 + (-$2,000) + $1,000] / 2 = $4,500 each. So, Debbie's net worth went from $10,000 to $4,500 and Bruce's net worth went from owing $2,000 to being $4,500 in the black.

If you have any questions, doubts or concerns, consult your attorney.

Name Changing

*If divorce has increased by one thousand percent,
don't blame the women's movement.
Blame the obsolete sex roles on which our marriages were based.*

– Betty Friedan

What's in a name?

In our society, it's customary for the woman to change her last name to her husband's once they get married, although it's becoming more and more common for women to choose to keep their maiden names.

Hyphenated last names - the bride keeps her maiden name and adds her husband's last name, separated by a hyphen - are gaining popularity as well. A relatively new trend is when both the bride and the groom change their last names so they match. (Example: Marilyn Johnson marries Douglas Evans and once married, they choose to become Marilyn and Douglas Evanson. Or, Susan Miller marries Charles Smith and they become Susan and Charles Smith-Miller.)

Still, although not required by any means, the most popular in our culture is the wife changing her last name to her husband's.

Some wives change their names without giving it much thought, just because "that's the way it's always been." Others choose to change their names so that the whole family unit, parents and children, share the same last name.

There are some women who feel that the last name doesn't make the family, and they feel strongly that their maiden name is part of their identity. These women don't want to lose that just because they're getting married.

There are some men who just happen to have funny, weird, or unpopular last names. Although the women marrying these guys love them, they want to retain their popular or easy to pronounce or spell last names.

On the other hand, just as many women have funny, weird, or unpopular last names. Many of these women who plan to get married can't wait to take their husband's last name.

I know a woman whose last name started with the letter "B" and her husband's last name started with the letter "W." Throughout her entire life she was accustomed to being at the "beginning of the alphabet," and couldn't fathom suddenly being at the rear or the end of the alphabet. So, she chose a hyphenated last name in order to keep her position at the beginning of the alphabet.

Changing, not changing, or hyphenating a last name once married is a personal choice and should be discussed before marriage. A groom may be proud of his last name and feel strongly (or simply assume) that his bride will want to take it as well, but in the back of the bride's mind, she may have other plans. (And although unconventional in our society, there is nothing wrong with the groom changing his last name to match his bride's last name. In many cultures, the maternal lineage is the significant lineage. In a way, the man taking his wife's last name would depict that. However, for the remainder of this section, let's assume it is the bride who will be changing her last name due to marriage).

It's these little things that can wreck a marriage before it's built a good foundation. By working out the little things in advance, couples stand a stronger chance of living happy long lives together.

Let's highlight some of the procedural tasks you'll need to consider if you're changing your last name. There are several legal documents you'll have to officially change. Such as:

* Your driver's license
* Vehicle registration
* Passport
* Social Security Card
* Mortgage loans
* Automobile loans
* Student loans
* Voter's registration
* Credit cards

* Bank accounts
* IRA / Investment accounts
* You'll have to alert the Human Resource department at your place of employment
* Insurance
* Beneficiaries
* Medical
* Professional licenses

There are several name change kits available online that can help you with all of the required forms you'll have to fill out and submit to various agencies in order to completely and legally change your name. As long as you are thorough, and follow the instructions provided in a step-by-step manner, you'll have no problem. If you're a very organized person, you can attempt to do it by yourself, otherwise it could get complicated.

Timing is very important when changing your name. For instance, you'll have to carefully coordinate your name changing effort with the first thing many couples do just after getting married – going on your honeymoon.

If you're flying away or cruising to your honeymoon destination, you'll have to be very careful. Let's say you're "thinking ahead" and you purchase your tickets using your husband's last name or your last name-to-be. (But what if you fail to think about changing your passport? Or what if the processing of your passport takes longer than expected or promised and does not arrive before your honeymoon?) When you arrive at the airport to board your airplane or the dock from where your ship departs you will hand the agent your ticket and your passport. If your passport has your maiden name and your ticket has your brand new married name, they won't match. Guess who's not going away on her honeymoon!

In this post-September 11th world in which we live, you literally may not be allowed to go on your honeymoon if you don't have the proper identification. Your travel agent or the airline or cruise line will probably prevent you from getting yourself into this pickle. If the agent is aware that it is your honeymoon, he or she will have the experience to alert and guide you toward the best way of handling the situation and probably just have you use your maiden name so that your ticket, passport, driver's license, visa and any other documents you may need will all be in sync. He or she may suggest that you hold off on your name changing effort until after you return from your honeymoon. If you make your own overseas honeymoon accommodations by purchasing your airline tickets, hotel accommodations, and rental car agreements or cruise line tickets over the Internet or by other means not associated with your travel agent, it'll be up to you to coordinate your name change so you're not left at the gate or the dock.

I've covered the most common legal matters in this chapter. However, depending on your individual situation, there may be specific things you should address that I haven't mentioned. It's always best to consult with your financial advisors and/or legal counsel before you embark on your marital journey to ensure that both you and your intended spouse are protected.

Questions to Ask Before Taking the Leap

1. If you uncovered things you weren't expecting during a background check, would you then ditch your fiancé because he or she is irresponsible?

2. Would you worry about the future of your own credit if you find out that your fiancé's credit history is poor?

3. Do you think the topic of a prenuptial will drive away your fiancé?

4. If you're the groom-to-be and your fiancée wishes to keep her maiden name, or use a hyphenated name, will that be palatable to you?

5. If you're the bride-to-be and you wish to keep your maiden name and you plan to have children, have you thought about what your children's last names will be? Would it bother you that your children might have a different last name than you?

6. If your credit rating is poor, would you be concerned about how it would affect your fiancés credit rating? Do you have a plan to improve your credit rating?

7. Is there anything you could or would do to protect your good credit?

8. If your fiancé wanted you to sign a prenuptial agreement would you? Why?

9. Does your philosophy regarding prenuptial agreements match your fiancés philosophy?

10. How important is it to have a good credit score? What do you think are the ramifications of having a poor credit rating?

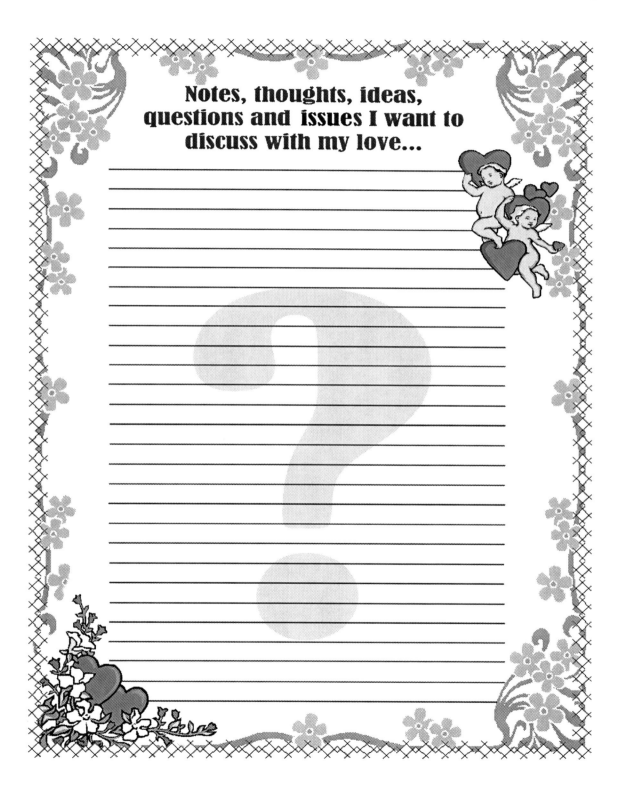

Notes, thoughts, ideas, questions and issues I want to discuss with my love...

Chapter Three

Single No More... What About the Rest of Your Life?

Don't smother each other. No one can grow in shade.

– Leo Buscaglia

Decision Making

*T*ransitioning from being single to being married is a major change in your life. When you take your vows, you're being asked to make a lifetime commitment to not only love, cherish and honor, but also to include your new spouse in every major decision you make. Me, myself and I changes to we, us and ours.

As an adult, you may be quite comfortable in making your own decisions. If you want to do something, you do it. If you're a single parent, not only are you accustomed to making decisions for yourself, you're responsible for making decisions for your child or children as well, and you may not be accustomed to asking someone for else's opinion on your purchases or anything else you plan for your yourself or your children.

When single, if you have a major purchase to make, it's your choice of whether or not to ask the opinions of close friends or family. However, if you want to make a major purchase - you do it. If you want to redecorate every room in your home – you do it. Decisions and choices you make are yours and yours alone and are not dependant on someone else's needs or desires.

The older you are and/or the longer you've been single, divorced, or widowed, the more set in your ways you may be. And frankly, you may like it that way.

But now that you're getting married, or are recently married, things are different - hopefully. Almost every decision you make, especially the major ones, will be made jointly with your life partner. It's not likely that you'll decide you need a new car and simply go out and make a purchase of that magnitude without first discussing it with your spouse. You'll both share in making decisions, not only based on your needs, but your spouses' needs as well.

Some newly married people find that they are resistant to this type of change and have a hard time collaborating on financial or other important matters. This may be somewhat normal.

To suddenly have to answer to your new spouse for decisions that you're not accustomed to sharing can be difficult at first. But this is a two-way street. Similarly, your new spouse has to answer to you for decisions that they are probably used to making on their own. I'm sure you wouldn't be pleased if you came home and your spouse was viewing his or her favorite show on a new wide screen, state-of-the-art, plasma television set; part of the brand new entertainment package that was purchased without your knowledge.

This new dynamic can and should be viewed as a positive thing. The sooner you are able to develop good communication on these topics, the sooner you'll be able to embrace your new marital status and negotiate your way through decisions that will affect both of you.

Finding a careful balance for this can be difficult in the beginning, but with commitment, it can be achieved. Your partner's expectations of married life may differ from your own. This is where patience and understanding will come into play to ensure that you both feel satisfied that you're working toward a common goal.

Things that can affect expectations are:
- Past relationships
- Education level
- Peers
- Family dynamics

How open is your fiancé's family when it comes to making decisions and communicating? What about your own family? It's important to realize that if either of your families don't communicate well or share in decisions, then you may naturally have challenges regarding communications in your marriage.

You don't have to jump in with both feet and turn all your decisions into a lengthy discussion before you're married. Start with baby steps in sharing decisions as your wedding day gets closer.

Planning for your wedding is a great way to start making decisions together. You'll find that major things like the budget for your wedding, the number of guests you plan to invite, and the number of people that will be in your wedding party, are all decisions that you will make together.

There are many decisions in planning your big day that the bride may make on her own, such as which of her friends or family will be bridesmaids, or the style and color of gowns they'll wear.

The groom will have decisions to make on his own as well, such as who will be representing him as best man, who will serve as ushers and the choice of groom's cake. Some grooms even decide the style of the tuxedos, shirts and ties for the men in the wedding party, although this will depend heavily on the style and color of the bridesmaid's gowns.

The decisions that will be made by one partner or the other will still be made within the overall parameters or constraints that you both have decided upon. Yet they still should be communicated or shared between both of you. For instance, if you've decided that the wedding party will include eight others (four bridesmaids and four ushers), the bride-to-be will select four women and the groom will select four men.

Of course you'll share who you've selected with each other. But you wouldn't decide that you absolutely need six people beside you when you take your vows without first asking or sharing this significant change in plan with your fiancé.

Likewise, if you jointly decide that your wedding budget will be $20,000, yet you estimate that you'll most likely spend in the neighborhood of $35,000, you'd have to let your fiancé know that you're way over budget.

How well you communicate while making these important wedding decisions will be a barometer, of sorts, to your ability to communicate in your marriage. Start sharing in decisions before the big day and it will be much easier to adjust to married life after the "I do's."

It may be easier to think of your fiancé as a life PARTNER and not a wife or husband. If you were going into business together, wouldn't you share in every major decision? Wouldn't that be a stipulation in your partnership?

Be honest, open and up front about your needs and desires in your decisions and discuss the reasons for surpassing your wedding budget and your desire to invite fifty additional guests. By explaining, discussing and planning these things before you're married, you'll have a good indication as to how your partner will accept change within your marriage.

I Want to Be Married
But I Don't Want to Lose My Identity

Marriage has the potential to erode the very fiber of your identity.

– Kristin Armstrong, Lance Armstrong's ex-wife

Believe it or not, this is a common fear, especially among women who plan to change their names after marriage. They were comfortable in their role of being "daddy's little girl" or "mommy's helper" and then transformed themselves into independent businesswomen with their own residence, bank accounts, and identity. Now suddenly, with the prospect of marriage they realize that the independence they've gained will be stripped away with the taking of their vows, and they'll instantly be known as "Joe's wife" or "Mrs. Johnson," and no longer as the independent individual they had worked so hard to become.

Soon-to-be husbands struggle with the same feelings, but perhaps on a lesser scale. Most men aren't faced with the decision of whether or not to give up the name they've had since birth. And the majority of men are not faced with the decision to have children and stay home to raise a family verses remaining in the "rat race" and earning a living. Though for some men, the thought of giving up their bachelor lifestyle is what keeps them from taking the leap into marriage. They've referred to themselves and thought of themselves as bachelors since they broke free from the apron strings and to tie the knot means giving up their bachelorhood.

Although marriage does change the way the world views a man and a woman (they're thought of as a couple instead of two individuals coming together with a common goal and a common bond), there is no reason you should have to lose your individuality.

Think of it this way: saying "I do" to another person does not automatically create a single mind. You're still an individual with likes, dislikes and desires that are separate from your partner's. Therefore, it's imperative to create a happy, healthy, harmoniously balanced marriage, while maintaining all that makes you unique. It is important to continue to strive for what you want out of life, independent of what your partner wants, as long as it doesn't interfere with your common goals and your marital vows.

Start by creating a list of things that you want out of life. Ask yourself: "What do I see myself doing five years from now?" Answer the question by creating a response list focused on that person you call "me." Don't include your children or your soon-to-be spouse in this list. To help achieve this, follow-up with additional questions to yourself: Do you love to paint or do you enjoy sports? What activities, hobbies, or interests do you want to keep as you go through life with your spouse? Oftentimes, these important things get lost somewhere along the way and create a feeling of loss or separation from the things you once loved to do. Sure, it's important to grow with your spouse as a couple and to experience life together through hobbies or activities, but it's just as important to continue to do the things *you* enjoy doing throughout your marriage.

Keep in mind that it's the things that you do in life, as well as how you think about the world and yourself that attracted your fiancé in the first place. If you give up those things to become like the person he or she is, then you'll lose your identity in the process and become somebody you no longer recognize. This is one area in which many relationships get off track. You take your vows as two individuals with completely separate lives, but lose yourselves in trying to please your partner. You'll wake up one day, 10, 15, or 20 years down the road missing the person that you once were.

Maintain your individuality by finding time to do the things that make you, *YOU*. Simultaneously, participate actively with your partner, doing things that bring pleasure to both of you. You'll grow together as a couple and both of you will grow separately, as individuals. By continuing to nurture yourself, you will not feel as though you lost yourself. You'll still be the person you were when you got married, only so much better.

My Spouse is Crowding Me. He/She Wants to Do Everything Together Just Because We're Married.

What you are as a single person, you will be as a married person, only to a greater degree. Any negative character trait will be intensified in a marriage relationship, because you will feel free to let your guard down -- that person has committed himself to you and you no longer have to worry about scaring him off.

– Josh McDowell

As explained in the previous section, individualism is important to maintain throughout a marriage. If you have a fiancé who isn't of the same mindset and desires to be at your side every waking moment of every day, it's best to confront the issue before you take the leap, otherwise it could spiral out of control once you're married. Oftentimes, "clinging" starts out with small changes in his or her social habits and turns into a big problem before you realize what happened.

In the beginning of your relationship, it's natural to spend a lot of time together. While planning your wedding, you will, once again, spend more time doing things together than you would do on a normal basis, especially if the groom is involved in making critical wedding decisions.

Maintaining individual schedules during this time of change will help you to bring the aspect of individuality into your marriage. Here are a few tips to keep the peace while living your own life:

- Schedule a weekly "boy's or girl's night" where you and your fiancé make plans with friends, and without each other. See a movie, go to dinner, or participate in an activity that you enjoy with friends. This will not only allow you to "get away" from each other for a while; it will also help you to maintain friendships outside of your marriage.

- Give your fiancé a gift. I have a friend whose husband had no friends outside the marriage. He was feeling lonely, isolated, and bored. As a third anniversary present she enrolled him in a local boxing school and surprised him by taking him to his first workout when he thought they were going to dinner. She watched as he interacted with the other boxers, and he seemed to enjoy the stimulation. She paid for his member-

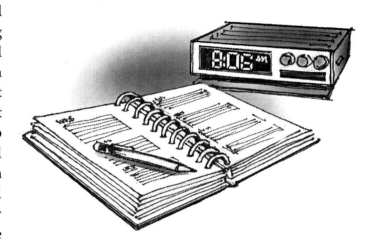

ship fee and signed a contract that night. Now, four years later, the boxing gym is his only get away. He still goes two nights a week, every week, and has something to do that is just for him. "It's the best present I could have ever given him." She told me. "It gets him out of the house two nights a week and he has something in common with the other boxers. He looks forward to going, and I look forward to having the house to myself while he's gone."

♦ Ask your fiancé's or your spouse's family and friends which hobbies they used to enjoy. If you're coming up with a blank as far as what he or she would enjoy, ask family members or long time friends what he or she found enjoyable as a child. Did he like to ride motorbikes? Did she dream of becoming a ballerina? We all have a secret wish of something we want to do when we "grow up" like my friend whose husband had a secret wish of becoming a boxer. Although he's too old to make it professionally, it's still something he enjoys. And although your fiancé may never become a ballerina or a professional motorbike racer, they may enjoy taking lessons or doing it as a hobby. Use your imagination and draw from the insight of those who have been around for years and figure out what your significant other would enjoy doing, outside of the house.

After you've been married for several years, issues may come up such as retirement, or the loss of a job, that may cause your spouse to lose sight of who they are and it may instill a need for security in the form of "clingy" behavior. They lose their identity, which may have been as the breadwinner, and seem to be lost and looking for their identity through you.

By working through these times together and openly discussing your separate roles in the marriage should one or both of you find yourselves unemployed, will alleviate any stress or anxiety that may arise at the thought of something happening in the future.

If your spouse has become clingy because of a recent job loss or career change, it will be beneficial to discuss the next step. Is he or she planning to look for a new job? Is it time to return to school for further training or to pursue interests in a new career choice? Discover what your spouse wants to do now, while being understanding of possible feelings of a loss of identity or a blow to his or her self-esteem.

Define Your Need for Space

*Marriage is that relation between man and woman in which
the independence is equal, the dependence mutual,
and the obligation reciprocal.*

— Louis K. Anspacher

When discussing your need for space with your spouse or fiancé, define what type of space it is that you need. Oftentimes, significant others will complain of smothering or feelings of not having time to themselves. But if you don't clearly define what it is you feel you're lacking, it may be construed as being pushed away or that you no longer desire to be with your partner.

Keep in mind the following when defining your need for space with your significant other:

* Define what type of space you need. Is it time to reflect, create, or self-discover? Are you feeling emotionally pinned or restrained? Do you need time with your friends once a week to play poker or mahjong or participate in your local photography club? Do you feel like you need one night away from home just to meditate, read a book, take a long bubble bath or listen to live jazz? Clearly define what you feel you're lacking in terms of space.

* Discuss your need for space BEFORE it becomes overwhelming. If you bottle up your emotions and your thoughts of being trapped, you may explode and say hurtful things to your partner or your partner may take your need for space as a form of rejection. Be open and honest about your personal needs before they escalate.

* Reiterate to your partner that your need for space has nothing to do with them and that your relationship is fine; it's just a personal need. Spend time with your spouse and show your love through appreciation and respect and realize that your desire to have personal space away from your mate doesn't mean that you no longer

want to be in the relationship. It's okay to get away from time to time and it's okay to consent to or support your partner in doing the same. Just because you're experiencing a desire to have some time for yourself does not mean your relationship is in jeopardy.

* If your partner is asking for space or time to do things with his or her friends without you, that doesn't mean you're no longer loved. So don't take it personally.

* Never gauge your relationship by someone else's. Just because John Smith, down the street, wants to spend every waking moment with his wife and he's happiest when he's by her side doesn't mean that your husband doesn't love you because he desires time alone.

How to Give Space

Now that you realize it's okay to have space and you know how to clearly define what it is that you need, let's review how to give space to your partner. How you give space will depend on what type of space your partner desires. For instance, if it seems you and your significant other share the same close proximity day in and day out because of close quarters, you both work at home, etc., work together to create your own separate areas. If you share a home office, place a divider in the room, make a schedule of times each of you will use the office, or set up a separate office area in another room in your home. If you are physically separated, if even by a wall, it will create an illusion of personal space.

If your spouse is feeling emotionally crowded, create a quiet environment and be respectful while he or she is reading or desires quiet alone time. You can do this by going to another room or going for a walk and allowing your partner to have time alone without interruptions.

To give financial space, set up a separate checking account for "fun" money that will not be accounted for in your budget. One of the biggest causes of arguments in a marriage is money, and by planning ahead for funds that can be unaccounted for, you and your spouse will feel free to make those small impulse purchases, without the anxiety that usually accompanies them.

The most important thing to remember is to be considerate of your spouse's feelings when it comes to personal space. If you desire constant attention and your spouse is a loner, don't take it personally when you're left on your own while your spouse enjoys their space. We're all different. We all have different likes, dislikes, and desires, so just be respectful of your spouse's wishes while remembering to not make personal sacrifices in your own needs for personal space and keep the lines of communication open.

Communication / Flexibility / Compromise / Negotiation

Only two things are necessary to keep one's wife happy. One is to let her think she is having her own way, the other, to let her have it.

– Lyndon B. Johnson

You are likely to face challenges as you navigate through this huge transition. The keys to making joint decisions are communication, flexibility, compromise and negotiation. These four elements are essential to making good decisions together.

These may sound easy and sensible. But for many people, the longer you've been single and making decisions on your own, the more difficult it may be to develop and live by these guidelines.

However, as you develop these characteristics you'll find that making decisions together will become easier and more natural to you.

Make it a practice to communicate with openness, honesty and forthrightness to your partner. Your fiancé probably won't understand your reasoning behind inviting an additional 50 guests at the last minute unless you explain the situation and discuss it.

Be flexible and compromise with your partner. This world is full of change and those who are rigid don't get very far. Dealing with someone who believes in the "It's my way or the highway" mentality gets old quickly. Getting along with someone who thinks, acts, and feels differently than you do requires both of your willingness to be understanding and flexible.

Negotiation is the key to change. It doesn't always have to be all of what you want or all of what your partner wants. If you are rigid in your decision making and make up your mind that you want an expensive entertainment center and your partner will have to do without a new couch, you might not end up with either. But you probably will end up with lots of anger and resentment.

Be willing to meet your fiancé half way. Be willing to settle for the less expensive entertainment center if your partner agrees to purchase the reasonably priced couch. Neither one of you may end up with the exact item you set out to purchase, but you can purchase the item you really want later down the line when you have saved up enough money to do so. Brainstorm. Jot down a list of off the wall possible solutions then blend or merge some of them together. Learn to be creative in your negotiating. It'll go a long way.

Compromise is what it's all about; you give a little, and your partner gives a little. Meet each other halfway, communicate, and realize that once you marry, it's no longer all about you. It's what works for your new family that counts.

The following are a few steps to help you communicate more effectively with your spouse:

- Establish a time to talk that is convenient for both of you. This is a huge obstacle among couples who both work or have busy schedules. Set aside time each week to "clear the air" or discuss what's going on in your lives. Make sure that you don't just focus on the negative, but have positive things to say as well.

- Listen to what your partner is saying. Make sure you truly understand his or her feelings about a subject and what's actually being said before you discuss possible solutions or try to "fix it."

- Focus on the ultimate goal and not picking a side. If you or your spouse is competitive, you may lean toward a stance that is opposite of what your spouse chooses, just for the sake of arguing. Keep your eye on the ultimate goal of the conversation, not the competition of who's right. Stay away from debating and learn to dialogue instead.

- Don't include "you" or an assumed "you" in every topic. Don't point the finger of blame. Use "*I*" statements. For instance, instead of saying, "*You* never take out the trash," change your tone to a positive one by saying, "I would like it so much if you would help me by taking out the trash." Just by taking the "*you*" followed by something negative out of your speech, you will sound like less of a nag and more like someone who is simply expressing his or her opinion.

It has been said that negative communication is carried out five times more often than positive communication within relationships. Work on the effectiveness of the communication in your relationship by keeping track of how many positive things you say versus negative. If you find that what comes out of your mouth usually starts with negativity or most of what you say has to do with something that isn't being done right, change the way you look at what's around you and focus on positive things, remarking on each one. You'll notice a tremendous change in not only the way you see the world, but also the way the world sees you.

Questions to Ask Before Taking the Leap

After each scheduled conversation, test yourself to see if you communicated and negotiated effectively by asking yourself the following questions:

1. What did I learn during our conversation?
2. Who did most of the talking?
3. Who did most of the listening?
4. Were there any interruptions, or were we respectful of what the other had to say?
5. What did I forget to ask or say?
6. Did we explore each topic thoroughly?
7. Did I acknowledge his or her feelings?
8. Was there anything left unsaid?
9. If you are concerned about maintaining your identity now that you're married or are about to be married, what can you do to maintain "yourself?"
10. Would you want support from your spouse?
11. How could your spouse support you?
12. If your spouse were concerned about losing their identity now that they are, or are about to be, married to you, how would that make you feel?

Notes, thoughts, ideas, questions and issues I want to discuss with my love...

Chapter Four

Finances

We can loan you enough money to get you completely out of debt.

– Seen On a Bank Sign

Issues involving money probably rank as the number one reason for tension in a marital relationship, and often are the source for separations and divorce in the United States.

Knowing this fact, how do so many couples fall into the trap of having money problems? More importantly, how does a married couple avoid the money pit?

First, you must understand the reasons why money issues cause such problems. The amount of money a couple has probably has little or no bearing on whether or not they will have money problems. You might think that couples who earn a substantial living and live in the middle class range or above may be less likely to argue and have disagreements over money.

Similarly, you might assume that couples who earn below a middle class standard of living and struggle to make ends meet each month may be more likely to argue and fight over money issues.

But, a couple's income and net worth are not necessarily the most important factor that causes disagreements over money issues.

Some things that may be more significant are:

1. the difference of how each partner relates to money, and
2. the impression each partner has of their income and their net worth.

What if, while growing up, John learned to buy only the top designer brands, to make impulse purchases, and to shop until he dropped? Also, John feels that as long as he hasn't reached his limit on his credit cards and/or as long as he has blank checks in his checkbook, he has money? What if John makes significantly more than his parents or his peers? Or, what if John perceives his financial self as privileged, wealthy, or rich or as the saying goes, "born with a silver spoon in his mouth?"

While John desires to maintain his lavish lifestyle to which he has grown accustomed, what if Sally grew up and, for whatever reason, learned that "a penny saved is a penny earned." What if she has taken on the practice of holding on to her money as long as possible? Sally has developed the mindset that a less expensive car gets her from point A to point B just as well as a top of the line, luxury car and doesn't pay for anything unless it's with a coupon, on sale or wholesale.

Sally perceives her financial self as not necessarily broke, but perhaps a little underprivileged or of lesser or meager means. She feels that in order to have the future she desires, she has to save aggressively. And she may feel this way regardless of her income level or that of her family's.

If John and Sally get married, even if they are in a high income bracket, they have a vast difference in their respective relationships to money and the value of money.

What do you think is likely to happen to this couple if they don't recognize these differences and discuss how they will relate to money as a couple after they get married? Well, we don't know exactly what would happen to this hypothetical couple, but at a minimum, they probably would have lots of tension regarding money concerns and financial decisions. And, if they separated or got a divorce, they certainly wouldn't be the first (or the last) couple to break up because of their different opinions of how to handle money.

Many times, money problems are just the symptom and not the real, underlying issue. A couple may find themselves arguing over money, and money is not the true issue that's at the root of the argument. Sometimes, the real problem is the fact that one partner has a control issue and the control issue surfaces and raises its ugly head when discussing money. (This control issue will likely show up in other areas too but you'd better believe it'll show up regarding money!) Although a couple argues about money, the underlying problem may be that of something completely different on the part of one or both partners.

For instance, what if one spouse is a stay-at-home mom or dad, or works outside the home but earns significantly less than their partner? The person earning the lesser amount or no income at all may feel that every time something needs to be purchased, he or she has to ask the other partner for money to spend. That could very well make them feel *dependent* upon the "breadwinner" for everything.

In this same scenario, the partner who's the "breadwinner" may feel like they are, or should be, in control of all finances because they earn the most. If this couple finds themselves arguing about money all of the time, money may not be the real underlying reason for conflict. It could very well be that control issues or dependency issues on either one or both sides of the relationship are the real problem.

But, instead of addressing the true issue of dependency or controlling behavior, they find themselves arguing about money time and time again.

The following are seven tips that will assist you and your partner, not only to controlling your spending, but also to ensure that you're on the same page when it comes to money in your relationship.

1. Figure out how you and your partner like to spend. Are you both spenders? Are you savers? Or do you avoid money topics and dealing with money like the plague? How do you handle money? And better yet, how does your partner? Will the differences in the way you handle money interfere in your relationship? Sure, it's easy to say you can make it through anything now, but what about when the bills are due and there isn't enough in the bank to pay them? Will the saver blame the spender in your relationship for lack of money? Have an honest, open discussion about each of your views about money and make a plan to control your finances as a partnership, not a dictatorship.

2. Make a list of your goals for your lives. You will hopefully be spending the rest of your days together, so you financial goals should be similar. With set goals, you'll be able to better manage your spending and work toward the same objectives throughout the years. Revise your goals on an ongoing basis, especially as your life situation changes.

3. Discuss your financial situation on a regular basis. Don't approach the subject with hostility or resentment. Instead, make a date of it and in a relaxed setting go over where you currently are and where you plan to be in the future. Be open-minded to suggestions and honest about your spending habits. Educate yourselves about finances and how money works. Excessive spending can easily creep into your marriage if left unchecked. Keep spending under

control by discussing your financial situation and revisiting your goals on a regular basis.

4. Make a budget. We'll cover this in the next section, but it's very important to have a budget and to stick to it as much as possible. As long as you're following a budget, neither partner will be able to blame the other for lack of finances.

5. In your budget, make allowances for entertainment. If you save every extra penny that comes into your household and don't take the time to enjoy life while you can, you may find yourself blaming your partner for your lack of fun. So don't forget to make a plan for enjoyment, while still saving.

6. Make a plan to share in the responsibilities of your finances. If one partner assumes the total responsibility, knowledge and control of the checkbook while the other has to ask for money in order to purchase anything, there could be a tug-of-war in the future for power.

Although it may not seem possible now, when little things start to build up in your marriage the power struggle could become your downfall. So make a plan before the wedding and stick to it.

7. Allow for petty cash. Each partner should have some "pocket money" to use as they please. Wives may want to purchase new shoes, go to dinner with their girlfriends or get their nails done, and husbands might enjoy golfing, taking in a live sporting event with their buddies, or other activities; thus, an allowance will alleviate having to account for every dollar spent on such things.

* Tip! Right now, take out your wallet, empty the contents and make copies of both sides of your license, credit cards and other important documents. While you're at it, get your passport and marriage license and make copies of those as well. Store these in a very secure place outside of your home – perhaps in a bank safety deposit box.

Budgeting

A good marriage is at least 80 percent good luck in finding the right person at the right time. The rest is trust.

– Nanette Newman

I'm not saying that you absolutely have to have a budget. But you know what they say about people trying to get somewhere without a map - they'll end up lost!

Let's face it, you're combining two households. It's similar to combining two corporations; two entities. There will be so many new variables regarding your combined finances. Some you've thought about, others you won't think about until you put forth the effort to budget.

Budgeting puts all of your concerns on paper; in black and white. All of your bills and expenses along with your income whether from one source or from multiple sources, are planned out so that you make sure your bills are covered and you have plenty left over to save.

If you don't budget your money, you're probably spending more than you realize. The art of establishing a budget allows you to understand your money flow, which is extremely important. It's important in the early years of your marriage and it will continue to be important throughout its duration.

Your needs will be different throughout your marriage. However, maintaining a budget will continue to be important in order to meet the needs of your future family.

Budgeting should not be thought of as difficult, arduous, or limiting. That's a negative way to think of something that can be a significant aid in helping you achieve your goals.

Instead, it's actually liberating in the strictest sense of the word. It's quite beneficial. Designing a good budget, and following, it can release you from your propensity of making poor financial decisions. It can heal a dire state of poor financial status as well as make a good financial situation better. When budgeting catches on and is embraced, rather than despised, it will be both energizing and invigorating.

For instance, if you know that you're prone to impulse buying, a budget doesn't mean you can't ever have some of the nice things you see when you're out "window shopping." It means that you can choose to have them when you can afford them. You'll be able to make an intelligent decision while truly understanding how much that impulse item is costing you.

Impulse buying may cost you the ability to pay down your mountainous credit card bill. It may keep you from saving for the car you desire. Or it may even cost you from saving for your dream home. Having a working budget makes it wonderful to put down that impulse item, knowing that this action is a step in the right direction to achieving your goal(s).

Without the benefit of having a budget, you'd never know how much that impulse item is actually costing you. Before budgeting, you may think the impulse item costs $100. But when you have a budget and understand your goals and your cash flow, you'll see that the impulse item is actually costing you the ability to achieve your dreams and goals.

Budgeting also prioritizes your spending. That means when you get your paycheck or money from income sources, the first thing you'll want to do is pay yourself. Invest in yourself. That may mean putting money away in an employer sponsored retirement plan (for example, a 401K plan) or contributing to your savings fund for your dream home. [This is the point where you want your money to work for you – instead of having to work for your money.] (For those of you who tithe, paying yourself may be second in your order of priority)

Next, work on building your cash reserves or emergency funds or contingency funds. How much do you need in cash reserves? Most professionals say you need at least three to six months of your salary saved in your cash reserves. See your financial advisor for help regarding building your cash reserves.

The next order of priority is to pay your bills. That includes, but is not limited to, paying your rent or mortgage, utility bills, car note and insurance payments. You'll also need to set aside money to pay for groceries and clothing

– (clothing that you need that is, not clothing that you want just because it's the latest fashion).

If you have children, you'll need to set aside money to take care of their individual needs. (I'm not talking about the latest electronic gizmo, gadget or toy, either!) Children's needs usually include things like school clothing, athletic gear, school supplies, medical, dental, orthodontist and optometrist visits, day-care, allowance and anything else that is a necessity for your child's health, education, or well-being.

When you have children, budgeting really helps keep your family on a clear financial track. It is difficult as parents to resist making impulse purchases especially when your children use the phrase, "all my friends have one."

Your budget will also help you understand whether having a cable bill and/or a cell phone bill of more than $200.00/month each is your best choice (Whoever said "talk is cheap?"). A budget helps expose these leaks in your financial situation and sheds light on your spending habits. Ask yourself: *Where do you want your hard-earned money to go? Would you rather have all the top channels on your satellite dish or cable network or put $100 or more away each month towards one of your previously defined financial goals? Do you see more value in spending your money on disposable items that will be used up and gone within the next few days/weeks/months or years or do you want to invest in your future?*

The lack of a budget is analogous to driving your car without a steering wheel, or trying to navigate a boat without a rudder. You'll end up wherever the water currents take you, having no means to steer towards the direction you want to go. Without a budget, you won't understand why you just don't seem to have any money at the end of the month. It won't make sense to you why you always have to borrow money or purchase so many items on credit.

You'll find yourself saying things like, "I make a good salary; why am I always in debt?" Or, "I make more than my brother. Why is my financial situation so much worse than his?"

Guess what? Ninety-nine percent of the time you'll have spent your money on stuff that you can't even recall a week, month, or year later. It goes fast and you won't even realize it.

Think about it. If you added up all of your receipts at the end of the year, how much do you think you would have spent on things such as dining, entertainment, groceries that went to waste or clothing that's hanging in your closet with the tags still attached? Do you think you wasted hundreds? Thousands? Tens of thousands? How much do you think you spend in a day, week, or month on nonsense items?

If you had a budget, you would know where every dollar went last year and you would be less likely to purchase more groceries than you can possibly eat or clothing items that you didn't really love, but just thought you may wear someday. And what about all of those expensive dinners or all the stuff you bought that you can't even recall what was on your mind when you purchased it?

After you develop a budget and adjust your lifestyle accordingly, you may be prompted to ask yourself the questions, "Do I really need that?" "How is that item going to help me?" "How is that item going to benefit us as a newlywed couple?" You may think, "Maybe I'd better put down the item for now. Maybe the item, after thinking it over and discussing it with my fiancé, is truly desired." That's fine! That's great! You'll make that decision from a knowledgeable standpoint. And, you'll know that it is the correct decision for you!

Also, after developing a budget you will have a clear picture of how you spend your money. Although, before your budget you were perfectly happy with paying $200 per month for cable TV, you may discover that having access to hundreds of channels might not be all that it's cracked up to be in the grand scheme of things.

You'll discover ways of cutting expenses without feeling deprived. Maybe you could cut your cable bill significantly, perhaps in half or even better and still be satisfactorily entertained if you cut out the channels you don't watch on a regular basis. Or, maybe you could take advantage of a package deal where you could combine your cable TV, cable Internet, and add a digital phone for actually less than you originally paid for cable TV only. Or, maybe the savings on your original cable TV monthly bill could then be applied towards other more important bills or savings.

This is simply one example of how a budget can, and should, work for you. When you write your budget, you'll discover many ways that you can best utilize your resources.

As I've said before, a budget doesn't have to be a bad thing. It can also identify discretionary funds; funds that you agree that you can spend for whatever you like per month. Let's say your budget reveals that you give yourself $200/month to spend on whatever pleases you. That's freedom! Yippee! You can spend that $200 without guilt on whatever pleases you without worrying about neglecting your bills or other expenses. You have the assurance that your rent/mortgage, car note, insurance, credit cards, savings for yourself, etc. have been adequately taken care. And, you also know that you won't accidentally or unknowingly spend $750 in a month; totally messing up your finances like you used to do before you put your budget in place.

There are various sources to assist you in preparing a good budget. A good budget is a good budget when it is adhered to and revisited periodically. When there is a significant change in your income, expenses, goals or your family status, your budget should be adjusted accordingly.

Financial Planning

Marriage is the triumph of imagination over intelligence.

– Oscar Wilde

*W*hen is the right time to create a financial plan or utilize the services of a financial planner? NOW!!!

If you don't already have one, this is the perfect time because you're a newlywed couple, or will become one soon, and you're beginning a new life – together. Having a financial planner at this early stage in your marriage will give you a jumpstart in making sound financial decisions now and in the future. Establishing a relationship with a good financial planner can help you develop a detailed financial map that will aid you in achieving your financial goals.

First, if one or both of you have financial planners already, you'll have to decide whether to keep both or to only use one. If you decide to only keep one, you'll have to decide which one to keep. Do you keep hers or his? Whichever one you choose, you'll obviously have to provide your financial planner with an update of your new marital status, your new income, your new debt, your new beneficiary information, your new goals, etc.

Or, you may want to start anew and obtain the services of a new financial planner that will work with both of you as a partnership. Some couples may like this option because they will be equals in the eyes of the financial planner. Whichever route you choose, your financial planner should be a professional. Whether or not they had a relationship with either of you before your marriage, you should expect them to provide excellent services to both of you once you're married. Another option is to utilize one financial planner for all of your joint accounts while each of you obtain or maintain your own financial planner for your individual financial needs.

The bottom line is, when you select a financial planner, you should both have a high level of trust for whomever you choose.

Your financial planner, if he or she is any good, should expose you to several phases of planning such as helping with your budget, estate planning, savings, investing, tax planning, etc.

Your financial planner should also be able to teach you about finances. If you have any questions regarding your personal finances, you should feel comfortable asking him or her questions and receive adequate answers from someone who is willing to make time for you. He or she should also be able to decipher your financial statements and explain them to you in terms you understand. If your financial planner can't or doesn't like to answer your questions, or you're not happy with the service you receive for any reason, get another financial planner. Period! That is your responsibility. They are your finances! It's your future at stake! Don't risk your financial well-being out of loyalty to a specific planner or organization for fear of hurting their feelings.

You should be able to use your financial planner as a resource, but you should always maintain control of your finances. You should have the final word in where or how your money will be invested. Therefore, delay signing documents until after you get an adequate explanation of what you're approving. Don't allow your financial planner to bully you into investing in anything you don't understand and don't let your financial planner sign anything for you. By signing a Power of Attorney, you could be signing over your decision-making rights. So it's never a good idea to give a Power of Attorney to a planner, unless you have extenuating circumstances (such as if you travel constantly for business) and aren't available to sign important documents. Even then, make sure you list the circumstances in which they have authority to sign for you on the Power of Attorney. (Allowing your financial planner to sign for you would not only give him or her too much control of your finances, it may be illegal in certain cases.)

Investments

Love seems the swiftest, but it is the slowest of all growths.
No man or woman really knows what perfect love is
until they have been married a quarter of a century.

– Mark Twain

Your financial goals will change over the course of your married life. There are many factors that drive these changes. Your age, your children and their ages, your goals, your health, your income, retirement, etc. are examples of factors that can and will affect your financial goals.

Your investment strategy or philosophy may change as a result of your age and your goals. A younger couple may want or have the ability to invest in a more aggressive portfolio. They have the luxury of time on their side. They have plenty of years, a few decades, before they reach retirement age. They may have 30 to 40 years before they reach "retirement age." Kudos to those who start early!!! That gives them the opportunity to keep accumulating dollars or equity. They have comfort knowing and understanding that even in tough times, if and when the financial market stumbles, they have plenty of time to buy more shares and recover financially.

Also, for those couples who start saving and investing early in life versus those who wait until they've almost reached retirement age, the more significant the effect of compounded interest. Compounded interest can be your best friend. The more time compounded interest has an opportunity to work for you, the better off you'll be financially when ready to retire.

An older couple just starting to invest doesn't have the luxury of time. Although it's never too late to start investing, the investment strategy for an older couple will likely be very different than that of their younger counterparts. They may want to start with a more conservative investment strategy or philosophy. Actually, an older couple who has been investing for many, many years, similarly, still needs to change their investment strategy into a more conservative one; because they don't have the years it sometimes takes to withstand major fluctuations in the stock market. A serious downturn could devastate them and they could possibly lose a significant portion of their nest egg.

We've all heard of couples who have lost their investments due to a negative turn in the market. They may have had plans to retire after years of hard work, only to discover that due to their loss of financial capital, they have to continue working for many years to make ends meet. A conservative approach, with an emphasis on security, can alleviate much of this hardship. And a good financial planner can guide you through these and other financial challenges.

Three types of investments:

a) Cash, stocks and bonds – these are "paper assets" and are considered "passive" because once you invest, there is little more to do other than manage your investments.

b) Investing in a business – Businesses are designed to be "cash flow" machines. You can be an active partner who does work in the business or a passive partner who invests in the business while others operate it.

c) Real estate investments – these are tangible assets. Real estate investments build equity and provide non-cash tax deductions i.e. depreciations.

Savings vs. Investing

The bonds of matrimony are like any other bonds - they mature slowly.

– Peter De Vries

How do savings differ from investments? Savings can be thought of as money put away to satisfy relatively short-term goals. If you want a new car, and your goal is to purchase the car in the next year or so, that would be an example of a reason for saving. Or, perhaps you want to purchase a house and your goal is to have the down payment for the house in the next couple of years, you would save towards that goal.

On the other hand, if you have a newborn and you're smart and thinking about putting money away for their college tuition, in that case you have approximately 17 or 18 years until you need the money. That's a long-term goal and plenty of time to invest rather than save.

If you're 25, 35, or even 45 years old, and you're planning for your retirement; that would be an example of investment planning instead of saving. That would be considered a long-term goal. That is plenty of time to invest.

Another difference between savings and investing is, in savings, since it is a short-term goal, you absolutely do not want to lose your principal or your capital. You don't have enough time to recover from any loss to your principal. You can't afford to lose the money you have towards your short-term goal.

Let's say you want to purchase a new house and you want to put a down payment of $10,000 within two years. Your plan is to start with the $4,000 that you received in a bonus from work, or as wedding gifts. You plan to save an additional $250 a month for the next two years. ($250/month * 24 months = $6,000) Your best avenue would be to "save" your money in a safe, secure, highly liquid vehicle, like a CD (Certificate of Deposit) or a money market fund or municipal bonds, for instance. You would get a relatively low return of interest, but you would not be in danger of losing any of your principle, as long as you don't liquidate before the term length provided by the financial institution.

Now, if you had a long-term financial goal, like retiring in 30 years; that would be an example of investing for the future. In this situation, you have the luxury of time on your side. You could invest in the stock market or aggressive growth mutual funds in an attempt to receive a higher return on your investment, but with more risk. No one wants to lose any part of their investment, but it can and does happen. If this were to happen to you, it would not be as detrimental to your plan because you would have plenty of time to change gears in your investment strategy and work on a recovery.

So, these types of investments are more risky than a low-yielding CD or money market fund, but the benefit is that the rate of return would be much, much higher. The risk is higher but, in turn, the possibility of a greater return exists.

With a carefully thought out plan, one that would minimize your risk while maximizing your growth potential, you could invest for your long-term future goals and achieve them satisfactorily. You may want to consult your financial advisor. He or she will be able to determine your risk tolerance and suggest investment vehicles that are aggressive enough to likely get you the return on investment you want, but not so risky that you would be nervous and suffer from ulcers.

Debt

The sum which two married people owe to one another defies calculation.
It is an infinite debt, which can only be discharged through eternity.

– *Johann Wolfgang von Goethe*

If either of you have any debt, your best bet, in most cases, (and I'll explain why later) is to pay off your debt as soon as possible. If you have bad debt, paying off your debt first may be the best way to help out your financial situation versus putting money into savings or investments.

Why? Most debts come with interest, and the sooner the debt is paid, the less money out of pocket you'll pay over the long run. Therefore, paying your debt and paying less in interest will usually save you more money.

Consider that your debt comes with an interest rate of 10%, your bank is offering 4% interest for a CD and you have an extra $1,000 that you would like to invest. If you pay off your debt versus purchasing a CD, you would net 6% more.

Just think of how much you would save if you paid off your bad debt first and then focused on regular debts and then savings. The "bad" debt to which I'm referring is credit card debt, rent to own, and other high interest debt.

Credit Card Debt

A word to the wise; going forward, don't ever get into credit card debt again – unless it is absolutely imperative. Credit card debt is not a good thing. It's okay to have an emergency card that is paid off in its entirety each month that boosts your credit rating, but to live by purchasing everything on credit is not good.

What's the interest rate on your credit card? 12%, 16.9%, 18%, more than 20%? That's huge!!! Please use your credit wisely. Try at all costs not to get into credit card debt. The best way to use a credit card is to pay off your entire balance every month. (Whew, what a concept! Only buy what your can afford!)

If you have an outstanding balance and you can't pay it off every month, you should pay more than the minimum amount. If you only pay the minimum amount, it will take you a very long time to pay off your balance. During that time, the credit card company will charge you all of that interest. You'll be stuck in an abyss of debt and you could end up paying several times the original amount for your purchases if you continue to pay the minimum amount each month.

What if something happens and you lose your job or the company folds? What if you find yourself physically incapable of earning the amount you earned when you originated the debt? Things like that happen across the country every day to people who never saw it coming and are faced with bankruptcy as their only option.

No matter how tempting it is to purchase big ticket items on credit, you'd be better off saving for the things you really want and paying cash or purchasing it when you can truly afford it. Set a policy or a mindset that if you don't have the cash to purchase it, then you can't really afford it. Of course I'm not referring to things such as a home or a car for transportation. Those are necessities. A house is not only a necessity, in most cases it is also a great investment that can be re-sold and will yield more than its original value.

The things you want to avoid purchasing on credit are things such as grocer-ies, small electronics, movie tickets, gasoline and any type of item that will be used up quickly or will depreciate significantly over the course of its life. This is because once it's used up or it's time to replace the item, you will probably still have the debt which will place you even further into debt. You should never have to continue paying for an item that you no longer have or use. That's the quintessential definition of "bad" debt.

Pay down your debt. That should be your first goal in your joint financial planning.

Here's another tip – pay your bills on time!!! Don't ever pay late fees. Late fees add up to extra money out of your pocket that is placed into the deep pock-ets of the big bank companies and other financial institutions.

Now, of course this assumes that you can pay your bills on time. If you have the funds to pay your bills on time and you're just plain lazy to the point that you pay your bills late - that's what I'm referring to. If you don't have the money to pay your bills on time – unless you have suffered a personal tragedy such as a job loss, or a medical emergency, you may have put yourself into a bad situation by simply buying over your head.

If you consider the fact that all of the money you spend in paying late fees could easily be money that you could have saved or invested for yourselves, you're really losing out for your future by not paying bills on time.

If you haven't yet established credit, you should know that it is a funny thing. The more money you owe, the easier it is to borrow more!

This is a new era. At one point in our history, to buy something on credit was a bad thing. Now it's the norm.

What's even funnier is that it takes credit to get credit. Establishing credit is a process. You can't turn on a switch and instantly have a credit history.

It's usually easier to establish credit with a store credit card like Sears or a gas credit card like Shell. In many cases it is more difficult to get a major credit card like MasterCard or Visa without an established credit history, unless you get one from your bank.

If your bank offers a credit card, even though you don't have a credit history, go ahead and apply. If your bank honors your relationship with them they may decide in your favor. If they still deny your request, how about a secured credit card? It uses your balance in a bank account or CD, for instance, as collateral. Your credit limit is based on your balance. The bank knows you won't default or if you do, they have tangible recourse. They already hold enough of your money to cover all of your credit card debt. So they're more likely to extend a line of credit to you. This gives you a great opportunity to begin to build and establish credit over time. You'll start with a relatively small credit limit. When you prove that you're a reliable credit risk they'll extend more credit to you by raising your credit limit. Sometimes it won't happen automatically. You may have to ask for additional credit. Before you know it, credit card companies will constantly mail you pre-approved credit card applications. But, be patient. It takes time, not to mention good habits and discipline to establish and maintain good credit. And always remember to use your credit wisely.

This reminds me of when I had just graduated from college as an Electrical Engineer and traveling was part of my job. I was 21 years old and in need of a credit card to make my air, lodging, and car rental reservations, not to mention all of my other travel-related expenses. I didn't have a credit history, and I had to get a credit card immediately because my job required me to travel, and you can't make reservations without a credit card (Even worse...try making car rental reservations without a credit card AND being under 25 years of age!).

Luckily, there was a bank near my job, and the person who was responsible for credit card accounts was a good friend of one of my co-workers. She made me apply for a gas station credit card and took a risk and approved my credit card application. (Ever hear this? Sometimes it's not what you know, it's who you know!)

Now credit card companies are enticing college students by GIVING them credit cards without them having established credit! What happens oftentimes is that irresponsible college students go wild with their credit cards, not understanding or caring about how to properly use credit. By the time they graduate, their credit is shot! What a hard way to learn a life lesson at such a young age. It's unfortunate for those who begin their adult lives behind the financial eight ball.

Once you've established good credit, guard it! It takes hard work, discipline, and perseverance to build a good credit history. Things like co-signing on a loan for your best friend, or canceling a cell phone account or an apartment lease and walking away from paying the fees will be with you for the next seven years, at least! Think before you sign and if you can't afford to pay cash, think before you spend. Can you really afford it?

Good Debt?

Is there such a thing as good debt? Yep. An example of good debt or debt that makes financial sense to have and not necessarily pay off early is your mortgage (as long as you have a low, fixed interest rate, that is). If you have a low, fixed interest rate on a mortgage, and continue to pay it back on time each month without ever incurring late fees, you don't have to worry about paying it off early like you would other types of debt.

If you want to pay it off earlier, consider a 15-year, instead of a 30-year mortgage. Or pay one half of your mortgage bi-weekly, or every other week, instead of paying your normal monthly amount. In effect, you'll make 26 half payments or 13 full month payments in a calendar year – essentially making one additional payment each year. You'd be surprised at how much that will help to pay off your mortgage in less time.

See your bank, financial advisor or mortgage broker for details. It's not necessary or required to have the bank (or worse, a third party company) setup this payment plan for you. If you do, you'll have to pay additional fees, whereas if you're disciplined, you could simply do it on your own. On the other hand, if you feel as though you are not disciplined enough to setup and abide by a payment plan like this, but you still see the value in such a plan, then by all means have the bank setup the plan for you. It is much better to pay them whatever fee they charge and have the early pay-off plan set up in your behalf than to "save" the setup fee and not be disciplined enough to follow through on your goal to setup the early pay-off plan you desired.

Another example of good debt is your school or student loans. These, too, are typically low interest loans and from a financial point of view, would serve you better if you did not pay them back early. In general, borrowing a large amount of money with a small interest rate over a long period of time is an example of good debt. Better stated, good debt is debt held against assets that appreciate in value.

Goals

Never go to bed mad. Stay up and fight.

– Phyllis Diller, Phyllis Diller's Housekeeping Hints, 1966

Okay lovebirds, what financial goals do you have? Your goals will depend on your situation, your age, your parental status, your health, etc. There are many factors that determine which short and long-term joint goals you may want to work towards in your marriage.

Regardless of what goals you may have, or how long you think it will take you to realize them, share them with your financial advisor. You and your spouse, or your fiancé, can enjoy working together toward your goals. This can be rewarding, if done correctly, and can actually bring you even closer together as a couple.

Some of your goals will be short-term goals or goals that you hope to realize within a relatively short period of time, as long as you stick to your plan. Or they can be long-term goals that may take many years of planning and investing before they are achieved.

Couples who work together toward short and long-term goals enjoy a unique type of relationship. When you work together towards a goal, you are aligned. You may very well have to work out areas of disagreement along the way, but you'll have a single focal point driving you; a mutually desired aspiration.

Once the areas of contention are worked out and the goals are achieved, you will share a beautiful feeling of pride and accomplishment, and you will notice a closer bond in your relationship because you will have learned to count on each other and trust each other to look out for what's in the best interest of your family.

Your goals don't necessarily have to be limited to financial goals. Your goal may be to plant a garden together in the spring, or do volunteer work in your community. Your goals may include your children. Maybe you want to commit to taking a weekend trip once a month to expose your children to cultural events. Or your goal may be to insist on spending time together without the children. Perhaps your goal will manifest by hiring a babysitter in order to go out on a date, spending every other Friday night together, alone!

Financial Goals

401k/403bKeough/Simple IRA – Does your job have a 401k plan for its employees? If the answer is "Yes," you are hereby advised to participate in this plan. Many companies will not only have this retirement savings plan setup for your benefit, they will also match a certain percentage of your savings. That's "free money!" In addition to all of that, your 401k contributions are tax-deferred. That means you don't have to pay taxes on the amount of money you save each pay period towards your 401k plan.

Let's say you make $40,000 a year, and you contribute 10% of your earnings to your 401k plan. You will only have to pay taxes on $36,000 of taxable earnings each year. The $4,000 or more, if your company matches a portion of your contribution, that you earmark toward your 401k plan each year is tax deferred. It will enjoy the benefits of compounding, and you can defer paying taxes until you withdraw these retirement savings after the age of 59 ½. Your tax bracket may be different after retirement as well. In many instances, your tax bracket may be lower because you may not earn the full amount of your salary, as when you worked full-time.

In all candor, unless you have extenuating circumstances, you would be amiss not to take advantage of this retirement savings incentive program. As true with all investing, it's never too late to get started. Also true, the earlier, the better!

Saving for College for Your Children

Marriage is a meal where the soup is better than the dessert.

– Austin O'Malley

Many banks and financial institutions offer vehicles for saving for your children's college expenses. So does the federal government. The common theme in this and any other investment goal is "the earlier, the better – but, it's never too late." See your financial advisor for recommendations on methods to save and invest for college.

If you don't have a financial advisor, or would like to find out your college funding options on your own, I've compiled a list of helpful websites that give useful information about alternative ways to save for college and how to apply for government funding.

- http://www.savingforcollege.com/tutorial101   This site includes general college funding information and 529 plans.
- http://www.finaid.org   This is possibly the most comprehensive source for financial aid information, including scholarship searches.
- http://www.fafsa.ed.gov No matter which college your child attends, if they apply for financial aid, they'll be required to fill out this form. It can be filled out completely and submitted via the Internet.
- http://www.fastweb.com Even non-traditional students can find financial aid through this site.
- http://www.scholarshiphelp.org This site gives college cost estimates as well as scholarship help.
- http://www.collegesavings.org This site offers another 529 plan help tool.
- http://cnnstudentnews.cnn.com/2002/fyi/teachers. ednews/01/24/free.tuition.ap/index.html This site offers a free tuition program for students in Tennessee. There may be similar programs in your area.

* http://www.usnews.com/usnews/biztech/ articles/060408/8free_tuition.htm You can find details on other tuition free programs at this site.

Questions to Ask Before Taking the Leap

1. Do you know your net worth?
2. Do you know your partners net worth?
3. Do you have short-term and long-term financial goals?
4. Have you shared them with your partner?
5. Has your partner shared his/her goals with you?
6. Are your goals compatible?
7. Do you have a working budget?
8. Do you and your fiancé/spouse have a similar or compatible relationship with money and finances?
9. Do you and your spouse feel you are knowledgeable about finances?
10. Would you be willing to sacrifice certain "luxuries" which you've grown accustomed in order to build a healthier financial picture?

Homework: Do you understand dollar cost averaging? Do you understand compound interest? Can you explain the time value of money? What is rate of return?

It is important that both of you are knowledgeable in the area of finances. If one of you is more financially savvy, then bring your partner up to speed or get your partner up to speed by encouraging them to read or enroll in courses or seminars on this subject.

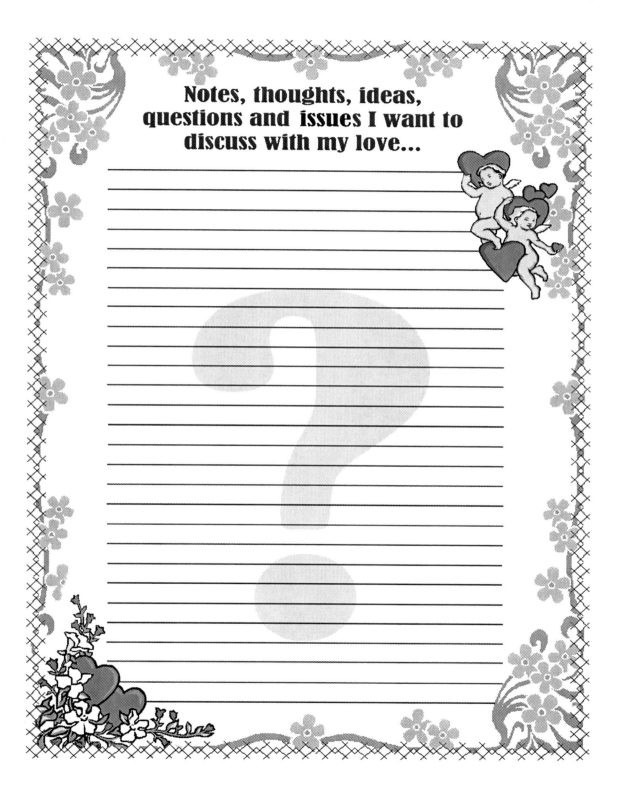

Notes, thoughts, ideas, questions and issues I want to discuss with my love...

Chapter Five

Health

After the chills and fever of love, how nice is the 98.6° of marriage!

– Mignon McLaughlin, The Neurotic's Notebook, 1960

*C*an marriage lead to a healthier life for both you and your spouse? Believe it or not, research studies have been conducted on adults who are married, unmarried, divorced, or living together, and they definitely show that married couples, particularly those who are married to their first spouse, live a longer, healthier life.

Well known sociologist, Linda Waite, and researcher Maggie Gallagher have said the following on this topic: "The evidence from four decades of research is surprisingly clear: a good marriage is both men's and women's best bet for living a long and healthy life."[2]

The University of Massachusetts conducted a study on health and marriage. Their conclusion was, "One of the most consistent observations in health research is that the married enjoy better health than those of other [relational] statuses."[3]

That's not all! One of the leading social scientists James Q. Wilson observed, "Married people are happier than unmarried ones of the same age, not only in the United States, but in at least seventeen other countries where similar inquiries have been made. And there seems to be good reasons for that happiness. People who are married not only have higher incomes and enjoy greater emotional support, but they tend to be healthier. Married people live longer than unmarried ones, not only in the United States but abroad."[4]

But wait! There is even more! According to Lois Verbrugge and Donald Balaban, people who are not married spend twice as much time in hospitals because of illness, and have lower levels of activity, than those who are married.[5] Dr. Robert Coombs' conducted similar research and found that "Virtually every study of mortality and marital status shows the unmarried of both sexes have higher death rates, whether by accident, disease, or self-inflicted wounds, and this is found in every country that maintains accurate health statistics."[6]

Professor Linda Waite, of the University of Chicago, in her 1995 presidential address to the Population Association of America stated that marriage has such great health benefits that a man who is married, but has been diagnosed with heart disease can be expected to live, on average, 1400 days longer than an unmarried man without any history of heart disease. That's almost four years longer for a married man to live who has a serious health problem, versus a man who is healthy, but not married.

What's even more amazing is that the life expectancy is longer for a man who is married and has been diagnosed with cancer or is over the suggested healthy weight by 20 pounds, compared to a man who is unmarried and of a healthy weight. Waite stated that this holds true not just for men, but women as well.[7]

Research has also proven that marriage:

* Provides both men and women the greatest levels of sexual pleasure and fulfillment.[8]

* Helps to protect women from both domestic violence, and violence in general.[9]

* Instills better eating habits, better self-care, and a more stable, secure and scheduled lifestyle.[10]

Married people recover from illness quicker, and as a result miss less work than those who aren't married. They are typically more stable in their employment, suffer from stress-related symptoms less often, are happier in general, suffer less from depression and loneliness, enjoy the role of parenting more, and have a lesser chance of abusing alcohol or drugs. In summary, they're more stable, happier and less co-dependant with a partner than their single counterpart.

If this mountain of research isn't enough to convince you that marriage is actually good for your health, think about the couples that you've known, perhaps your grandparents, who stayed married for years and lived long, productive, and happy lives.

Make a Health Plan

Let thy food be thy medicine and thy medicine be thy food.

– Hippocrates

Even though marriage, in general, can boost your life expectancy and your health, you should definitely make a plan with your fiancé to maintain a healthy lifestyle. One possible reason for losing interest in your mate is health related - obesity. The common mentality is that once you've found your partner, you no longer have to try to attract the opposite sex. This way of thinking, however, couldn't be further from the truth.

You've probably heard the saying, "Whatever you did to get them - you've got to do to keep them." It's true! Even though beauty is on the inside and people shouldn't judge a book by its cover, nobody wants to marry Cinderella and wake up each morning next to the ugly stepsister. (Or otherwise stated; nobody wants to marry Prince Charming and wake up each morning to fat Albert!).

I know this is a stretch in most cases, and I'm not suggesting you look as if you just stepped out of the salon 24/7 - 365. And I'm not saying that it's reasonable to expect that you maintain your weight and size from your wedding day until the day you retire. The point I'm trying to make is that packing on pounds, living in sweats, and no longer caring about your appearance can drive away your mate. Husbands have been known to do this as well as wives. The image of your husband lying on the couch unshaven, wearing a dirty t-shirt, beer belly exposed may not be as attractive as other images in your head. So make a plan before your wedding to take time out for yourself and do what you need to do to keep yourself attractive to your spouse.

Your plan should include a regular exercise routine and a healthy diet. The following are the suggested key guidelines for diet and exercise from the United States Department of Agriculture:[11]

Adequate Nutrients Within Calorie Needs

- Consume a variety of nutrient-dense foods and beverages within and among the basic food groups while choosing foods that limit the intake of saturated and *Trans* fats, cholesterol, added sugars, salt, and alcohol.

- Meet recommended intakes within energy needs by adopting a balanced eating pattern, such as the U.S. Department of Agriculture (USDA) Food Guide or the Dietary Approaches to Stop Hypertension (DASH) Eating Plan.

Weight Management

- To maintain body weight in a healthy range, balance calories from foods and beverages with calories expended.

- To prevent gradual weight gain over time, make small decreases in food and beverage calories and increase physical activity.

Physical Activity

- Engage in regular physical activity and reduce sedentary activities to promote health, psychological well-being, and a healthy body weight.

- To reduce the risk of chronic disease in adulthood: Engage in at least 30 minutes of moderate-intensity physical activity, above usual activity, at work or home on most days of the week.

- For most people, greater health benefits can be obtained by engaging in physical activity of more vigorous intensity or longer duration.

- To help manage body weight and prevent gradual, unhealthy body weight gain in adulthood: Engage in approximately 30-60 minutes of moderate to vigorous-intensity activity on most days of the week while not exceeding caloric intake requirements.

- To sustain weight loss in adulthood: Participate in at least 60 to 90 minutes of daily moderate-intensity physical activity while not exceeding caloric intake requirements. Some people may need to consult with a healthcare provider before participating in this level of activity.

- Achieve physical fitness by including cardiovascular conditioning, stretching exercises for flexibility, and resistance exercises or calisthenics for muscle strength and endurance.

Food Groups to Encourage

- Consume a sufficient amount of fruits and vegetables while staying within energy needs. Two cups of fruit and 2½ cups of vegetables per day are recommended for a reference 2,000-calorie intake, with higher or lower amounts depending on the calorie level.

- Choose a variety of fruits and vegetables each day. In particular, select from all five vegetable subgroups (dark green, orange, legumes, starchy vegetables, and other vegetables) several times weekly.

- Consume three or more ounce-equivalents of whole-grain products per day, with the rest of the recommended grains coming from enriched or whole-grain products. In general, at least half the grains should come from whole grains.

- Consume three cups per day of fat-free or low-fat milk or equivalent milk products.

Fats

- Consume less than 10 percent of calories from saturated fatty acids and less than 300 mg/day of cholesterol, and keep *Trans* fatty acid consumption as low as possible.

- Keep total fat intake between 20 to 35 percent of calories, with most fats coming from sources of polyunsaturated and monounsaturated fatty acids, such as fish, nuts, and vegetable oils.

- When selecting and preparing meat, poultry, dry beans, and milk or milk products, make choices that are lean, low-fat, or fat-free.

- Limit intake of fats and oils high in saturated and/or *Trans* fatty acids, and choose products low in such fats and oils.

Carbohydrates

- Choose fiber-rich fruits, vegetables, and whole grains often.

- Choose and prepare foods and beverages with little added sugars or caloric sweeteners, such as amounts suggested by the USDA Food Guide and the DASH (Dietary Approaches to Stop Hypertension) Eating Plan.

- Reduce the incidence of dental caries by practicing good oral hygiene and consuming sugar and starch-containing foods and beverages less frequently.

Sodium and Potassium

* Consume less than 2,300 mg (approximately one teaspoon of salt) of sodium per day.

* Choose and prepare foods with little salt. At the same time, consume potassium-rich foods, such as fruits and vegetables.

Alcoholic Beverages

* Those who choose to drink alcoholic beverages should do so sensibly and in moderation—defined as the consumption of up to one drink per day for women and up to two drinks per day for men.

* Alcoholic beverages should not be consumed by some individuals, including those who cannot restrict their alcohol intake, women of childbearing age who may become pregnant, pregnant and lactating women, children and adolescents, individuals taking medications that can interact with alcohol, and those with specific medical conditions.

* Alcoholic beverages should be avoided by individuals engaging in activities that require attention, skill, or coordination, such as driving or operating machinery.

Food Safety

* To avoid microbial food borne illness:

  * Clean hands, food contact surfaces, and fruits and vegetables.

  * Separate raw, cooked, and ready-to-eat foods while shopping, preparing, or storing foods.

  * Cook foods to a safe temperature to kill microorganisms.

  * Chill (refrigerate) perishable food promptly and defrost foods properly.

  * Avoid raw (un-pasteurized) milk or any products made from un-pasteurized milk, raw or partially cooked eggs or foods con-

taining raw eggs, raw or undercooked meat and poultry, unpasteurized juices, and raw sprouts.

You can also check out sites such as http://www.MyPyramid.gov and specify your age, sex, and amount of physical activity each day and it will give you a suggested meal plan to ensure that you include all of the necessary food groups in your daily diet. You can also print out a PDF worksheet to daily keep track of your activity and consumption.

Having a plan to maintain a healthy body will give you more control over the amount of diet and exercise you accomplish in any given day. Without a plan, the days may pass by and before you realize it, you could find yourself out of shape and in poor health. It's always better to work with a partner for motivation and inspiration. So make a plan to stay healthy together.

Here's to your health!!!

Questions to Ask Before Taking the Leap

1. Does your fiancé share the same health mindset as you?

2. Does one or both of you work out on a regular basis?

3. Do you share the same diet?

4. Is there anything about the way your fiancé cares for their body that you would change?

5. Is there anything that you need to change about the care of your body to ensure a long, healthy life with your partner?

6. Do you share the same mindset when it comes to health and exercise for your children?

7. Do you see health as a concern in your marriage?

8. Would you consider your diet to be a healthy diet?

9. What are three things you and your fiancé/spouse could do immediately to improve your health and/or your diet?

10. Do you and your fiancé/spouse get regular check ups?

11. Has your doctor offered advice that would help to improve your health that you've consistently ignored? Why?

**Notes, thoughts, ideas,
questions and issues I want to
discuss with my love...**

Chapter Six

Insurance

*Matrimony is a process by which a grocer
acquired an account the florist had.*

– Francis Rodman

Health

*I*nsurance, in general, is a very important, yet admittedly dry topic, and one that young couples oftentimes deem unnecessary. No matter your age or current health, it helps to think of health insurance as an imperative expense for two important reasons. First is the obvious – for regular health maintenance. Second, in the event of an accident or sudden illness, you'll need health insurance to provide the health care you'll require to get back on your feet. Without proper health insurance, you could find yourself in an overcrowded, under staffed hospital emergency room or clinic and may end up worse off than when you were admitted simply because you had to wait for hours to be seen.

Also, in the event of an accident or a sudden illness, the health costs you incur could potentially be so high they could put your financial situation in serious jeopardy. Many people in this country have lost everything; their homes, cars, savings, and everything else of value they own because they weren't prepared for illness or an accident. Living without health insurance is a recipe for disaster. It's like a trapeze artist flying without a net. (One false move and…) It's essential for families and although it can be costly, you really can't afford to live without it. Heaven forbid if you're stricken with a medical emergency, involved in an accident, require expensive medication, need an operation or become pregnant without health insurance. You could rack up thousands of dollars in debt, which could be avoided by planning ahead and paying a monthly health insurance premium.

There are several questions to be answered on this topic in order to decide what type of plan or coverage is best for you and your future family. Are you both employed, and does each of you have the option for a health insurance plan through your employer? If both of your employers offer a health insurance plan, how many dependants are you responsible for? If it's just the two of you (in other words, if neither of you have any other dependents), is it more feasible for you both to remain insured by your respective insurance plans; or would you prefer that both of you be covered by one health insurance policy?

In most cases, it would be better for each of you to keep your respective health insurance. It's less expensive for both of you to maintain an 'employee only' health insurance plan than either one of you to maintain an 'employee plus spouse' or an 'employee plus family' plan.

Be aware that changing health plans could possibly decrease your coverage because of "pre-existing conditions." If you or your spouse have a pre-existing condition, and you decide to change your health insurance provider, the new provider oftentimes will limit your new coverage, stating that if you have been diagnosed for a health condition prior to switching providers, that condition will not be covered by the new plan for a predetermined period of time. Make sure you fully understand your coverage and co-pay requirements before you switch plans. If there is an unplanned pregnancy, which isn't unheard of in newlywed couples, and it's the wife who has switched to the husband's plan, you will want to be sure that you'll be adequately insured if she becomes pregnant.

If you have dependants, you'll want to figure out which health insurance plan would best fit the needs of you and your children. To make that determination, you may want to weigh factors such as: deductibles; co-pays; emergency care costs; network providers; dental care; vision care, prescriptions; and coverage for major surgeries or prenatal care, especially if you plan to expand your family tree.

If you currently receive health insurance coverage from your employer, in order to even consider changing to a new plan you must have a "qualifying event." Health insurance coverage is based on a fiscal year. Once a year, just prior to the beginning of the new fiscal year, you'll have an opportunity to review and possibly change or revise your health coverage. This period is called the "open enrollment period." The only way you can change your health insurance coverage during the fiscal year, other than during the open enrollment period, is if you have a qualifying event. A qualifying event is a life event which enables you to change your health insurance plan or coverage in the middle of a year, instead of waiting for the annual open enrollment period. Examples of qualifying events are events such as: a new marriage or specifically a change in marital status, the birth or adoption of a baby, moving to a new geographical location, changing employers, etc. Consult your human resources department or benefits department at your place of employment for an exact list of qualifying events.

If only one of you works, or has health insurance offered through your job, then your decision is easy. The one who is working and receives health insurance through their job simply must cover the entire family.

If neither of your jobs offers a health insurance plan, or you're both self-employed, then you must purchase private health insurance. You'll have to shop around to ensure that you're getting the best coverage. Your financial planner may be able to provide you with assistance in locating a private health insurance provider.

Other things to consider…

You'll have a variety of types of health insurance plans to choose from. Some of the more common plans are HMO (Health Maintenance Organization – a type of group health insurance plan providing medical services though a group of doctors, medical personnel and medical institutions), PPO (Preferred Provider Organization – another type of group plan managed by an insurance company where doctors, medical personnel, and medical institutions provide health care), POS (Point of Service – which has many characteristics of an HMO or PPO), and HAS (Health Savings Accounts – a tax-deferred savings vehicle, like an IRA, used for medical expenditures.)

You'll want to learn the differences between these types of health plans so you can make an informed decision on which is best for you and your family. Your company's benefits department, human resources department, and/or the health insurance provider will be able to help you navigate your way through the health insurance options you face.

Most, if not all health plans will require you to have a PCP (Primary Care Physician or Personal Care Provider.) A primary care physician is a family practitioner or licensed medical provider who would be your main doctor. Your insurance plan will provide you with a list of which doctors in your area belong to the plan and would qualify as your PCP. If it's necessary for you to see a specialist, your PCP can refer you to someone who is in your group health plan.

Another issue to consider is whether you'll be responsible for the health insurance for others. Depending on your age and/or circumstances, you may be fully or partially responsible for your parent's health insurance, as well as your own. It's important to keep in mind who in your family (yourself, your spouse, children, step-children, parents, or any other dependants) you'll need to provide coverage for and what types of coverage will be necessary to provide the best medical care for your specific situation.

Pre-existing Conditions

Chains do not hold a marriage together. It is threads, hundreds of tiny threads which sew people together through the years.

— Simone Signoret

A pre-existing condition is any type of medical condition that you or your soon-to-be spouse has been treated for or have been prescribed medication for a period of time prior to applying for a new health care policy. The period of time can be as little as six months to as much as five years depending on various factors.

Insurance carriers will waive the pre-existing condition term of the policy after a waiting period. However, if the person with the pre-existing condition has had coverage for 63 days prior to obtaining the new policy, the waiting period will then be shortened. They're required by law to do so because of the federal Health Insurance Portability and Accountability Act (HIPAA).

Check with your insurance carrier or the human resources department of the insured's place of employment to determine if any pre-existing conditions will be excluded from your policy or if you will have a waiting period before they will be covered.

Home Owner's

A man marries to have a home, but also because he doesn't want to be bothered with sex and all that sort of thing.

– W. Somerset Maugham

If you own your home and you have a mortgage, you probably already have home owner's insurance. It's required by your mortgage company. However, consider this example:

What if the mortgage company requires that you have enough insurance to cover the amount of your mortgage? Let's do a little math - If you purchased your home for $150,000, and the amount of your mortgage is $120.000, that's great! Your equity is $30,000. Your insurance company would require you, at the time of purchase, to insure your home for the mortgage amount or $120,000. That's the amount of your mortgage, not the purchase price of your home. They only care that their investment is insured.

Now, if anything catastrophic were to happen to your home, such as a fire, the good news is that you're insured! The bad news is that your home was only insured for the amount of the mortgage, not for the fair market value of your home.

In this simplified example, the insurance company would send you a check for $120,000, which you in turn, would send to your mortgage company to satisfy your financial obligation. *But what about my equity?* Gone! Bye, bye Charlie! Up in smoke… pun intended!

The lesson here is even though your mortgage company requires that the minimum amount of home insurance you carry is enough to cover the mortgage amount you borrowed, you can purchase a larger home insurance policy. It may be worth your while to consider purchasing a home insurance policy large enough to cover the value of your home, as opposed to just covering the amount of your mortgage. In this example, you would have been wise to purchase home insurance in the amount of $150,000 versus the $120,000 your mortgage company deemed necessary.

Why doesn't the mortgage company recommend purchasing enough insurance to cover the actual value of your home instead of only the mortgage amount? Simple - They are concerned that you have enough home insurance to cover <u>their</u> interests, not yours. They, quite frankly, aren't concerned about your interests. You must be responsible to have enough insurance to cover your own interests – namely your down payment and home equity, as well as your personal belongings.

Also, keep in mind that as years go by and the value of your home appreciates; you'll want to get your home appraised to know its current value. Following the last example, let's say years down the road your home appreciates to $165,000. That means the value of your equity went up from $30,000 to $45,000 (plus the amount of mortgage principal you paid in five years). If you had a catastrophic fire destroying your home and your home was still insured for the original mortgage amount of $120,000, you would be out $45,000. Ouch!

Even if you were wise enough to insure you home for the original purchase price of $150,000 at the time of purchase, yet you neglected to update your home insurance policy to reflect the increase in equity periodically, you would still be out of $15,000 in this example.

If your home is damaged so badly that you can't live there until it's been repaired, you'll need to live somewhere temporarily until you can move back home. You can also purchase insurance to pay for temporary housing.

The previous example of home owner's insurance covered the value of the physical building; however, the contents of your home should be insured as well. You should add the value of your furniture, computer, electronic equipment, jewelry, clothing, artwork, etc. to your home owner's policy. What would happen if your home burned down tomorrow? You may have your home insured to cover your mortgage and your equity, but what about everything else? You'd have to start collecting new personal items and that can be costly.

You would also be very wise to keep your receipts, serial numbers, and even take pictures of your valuable possessions as documentation for the insurance company (Keep a copy of all of this valuable documentation in a safe or at a different location than your home. If you had a catastrophe, and you needed to produce this documentation, but you kept it in your desk drawer, err…you get the picture!)

If you live in a flood prone area and your home owner's insurance doesn't cover flooding you may want to consider additional coverage. Typically, home owner's policies do not automatically include flood insurance. If you live in a designated flood zone, your mortgage company will actually require you to obtain additional flood insurance. You may also want to consider additional coverage if you live in a humid or tropical area. Mold damage can be costly to fix and most policies won't automatically cover it.

Flood and mold damage insurance are not usually a part of a standard home owner's insurance policy. They are examples of additional or optional insurance coverage's called "riders" which can be added to a standard insurance policy at an additional cost.

You'll also want to consider any exterior items that may not be covered on your policy such as lawn equipment, portable buildings, tractors, detached garages, etc. Discuss all of your options with your insurance agent to determine what extra coverage, if any, you may need to purchase.

Now, if you have guests over to your home and someone slips and falls on your beautifully waxed floor and breaks their leg, they can sue YOU. They can sue you because they had an accident on YOUR PROPERTY. You'll need insurance to cover against these types of situations, too.

Tip – If you have an appraisal performed on your home examine the report. The appraised value of your home will be made up of two parts - the value of the land and the value of the building (your home). Only insure the value of your home – not the value of the land.

Tip – It has been stated, "I don't care if you live on Mount Everest, buy flood insurance." (Remember hurricane Katrina)

Renter

Sometimes I wonder if men and women really suit each other. Perhaps they should live next door and just visit now and then.

– Katherine Hepburn

Are you renting right now? If you and your new spouse are planning to rent an apartment, condominium or a house after you're married, you'll want to be sure that you have renters insurance. The owner of the house or the apartment building is required to purchase insurance for the dwelling so that if the dwelling burns in a fire, or takes on water due to a broken pipe or a flood, or someone trips and hurts themselves, it will be covered.

However, in the event of a robbery, if your computer or jewelry is taken and your television and artwork are damaged, you'll need to have coverage for the contents of your home. You'll need insurance protection for your personal possessions. Your landlord is not responsible for the protection of your personal possessions and will not provide insurance coverage.

If you own a condo, townhouse, or any type of shared dwelling, you'll need insurance to protect your personal belongings including the structural part of the building that you own, as well as a type of "master policy" that's usually provided by the condo or association board. This "master policy" will cover any type of shared space or common areas, such as the roof, floor, basement, hallway, elevator, lobby, boiler, walkways, etc. Usually this is included in your association fees.

Fires, floods and other disasters can cause a loss in these areas. Additionally, visitors who "trip" on loose carpeting or fall down a flight of stairs can sue those responsible for the upkeep of the shared areas. Having a "master policy" will cover any potential losses you may incur because of these types of scenarios.

It's a good idea to take inventory of all of your belongings. This serves multiple purposes. First, it will give you the best idea of how much renters insurance you need. Otherwise, it will be an estimate, at best. Many times, after it's too late, people will find out that they did not purchase enough coverage (The other side of the coin is the situation where you are over insured; paying too much insurance coverage than you need – wasting money unnecessarily).

Also, in the event of a fire or any other disaster that causes you to file a claim, having a good inventory makes your claim much easier to prove. If you have a description, manufacturer name and model, serial number, receipt, and a picture of each item you're claiming a loss on, that will make your claim so much better than if you have to rely on your memory after its gone or damaged. You'd be surprised at how much "stuff" you own. The value of your belongings may be considerably more than you'd imagine. Make certain that your inventory list is secured in a place other than your home because if you experience a disaster that destroys all or part of it, your inventory list may be lost or destroyed, too.

Auto

I have great hopes that we shall love each other all our lives as much as if we had never married at all.

– Lord Byron

here are several types of auto insurance. You'll want to discuss what types of coverage you'll need and how much of each type with your auto insurance agent. Some of the different types of auto insurance are:

1. Property Damage Liability – This insurance pays for the repair or replacement of damaged property, including the other person's car in case of an accident.

2. Bodily Injury Liability – This insurance is mainly to protect your assets from lawsuits in the event you're involved in an accident – even if the accident is not your fault.

3. Uninsured Motorist Protection – This protects you in the event that the other person is not fully insured or does not have any auto insurance.

4. Collision and Comprehensive – This pays for the repair and/or replacement of your car in the event of an accident.

5. Personal Injury Protection – This coverage is to pay for your medical costs in the event of an accident.

You and your agent will determine which of these types of insurance will be most beneficial to you. Most states require you to carry certain types of insurance, like liability. Other types of insurance may be optional, such as towing, roadside service, etc. Your auto insurance agent will be able to assist you as you navigate through your auto insurance needs.

If you and your spouse have different auto insurance companies, this may be a good time to consolidate your policies into one. Your annual combined premiums will likely decrease as a result. Auto insurance premiums for married women and married men are less than those of single women and single men. That means that even if you kept your respective auto insurance companies, the fact that your marital statuses have changed from single (or divorced) to married should result in a change to your auto insurance premiums as well.

Additionally, if you choose to combine your policies and use one auto insurance company, you'll enjoy additional savings. Most insurance agencies give multi-car discounts. In addition, insurance companies give you a bit of an incentive when more than one person in your household is covered.

Be sure to give both of your insurance agents a call to discuss the benefits of adding your spouse to your existing policy. You can then compare the quotes from both companies before you decide which will be the best route to take. Be sure that you're comparing apples to apples. Most times if your give your insurance agent an opportunity to increase your coverage, they'll try to sell you more than you asked for. That's not necessarily a bad thing. However, it wouldn't be a fair comparison if one company is quoting you on apples and the other company is quoting you on oranges. You won't know which company is quoting you the best price unless the coverage you're receiving is comparable.

Also, note that insurance companies may utilize tactics such as, "If you increase your coverage in this area, then you'll be eligible for additional benefits in that area. But, we can't offer you coverage in that area unless you increase your coverage in this area first." You'll just have to navigate through the seemingly impossible maze of information you receive. If you need outside help, don't be afraid to ask. Your financial advisor may be able to help you or refer you to a knowledgeable, trusted source.

(You may want to consider joining an automobile travel club for extra protection outside the scope of traditional auto insurance.)

Umbrella Policies

I have great hopes that we shall love each other all our lives as much as if we had never married at all.

– Lord Byron

An umbrella policy is a supplemental insurance policy which will provide coverage above and beyond what your home owner's, auto or other similar policies cover. The terms of coverage in an umbrella policy are usually much broader than that of your main policy, which allows you to possibly cover those things that your policy excludes.

Some consider umbrella policies overkill, but depending on your specific circumstances, the additional coverage may protect you in the event of unforeseen circumstances. A classic example is if your house succumbs to fire. Your home owner's insurance policy may cover the replacement of your home. But during the time it takes to replace your home, you may have to stay in supplemental housing. Your umbrella policy may cover the cost of your temporary housing during the time your primary residence is being restored.

Discuss your insurance options not only with your agent, but with your financial advisor as well. He or she will be able to guide you to pick out the best coverage for you.

Life

Marriage is not a word - it is a sentence.

– Author Unknown

Your employer may provide a minimal life insurance policy. Most employers will provide you with an insurance policy equivalent to your annual salary which includes an option to pay for additional coverage of up to four times your annual salary or more. Some companies will even allow you to purchase additional life insurance provided you pass certain requirements. But depending on the type of life insurance policy, it may merely be enough to cover funeral expenses. If your employer doesn't provide life insurance, or the life insurance your company provides is deemed insufficient by you and the needs of your family, then you can purchase a private life insurance plan.

You'll have to determine how much life insurance you need. *How do you calculate how much life insurance you need?* There are many factors that should be considered in order to calculate the optimum amount of life insurance for your situation. Start by considering how much your funeral may cost. If you have children, what are their educational cost requirements? What is your spouses' age and income potential? How much debt and how many assets do you have? How much would your family need in order to maintain their standard of living; over what period of time?

If you receive a raise, or get a new job, it may be necessary to reassess your life insurance needs at that time. At this point in your life, while preparing for marriage, $50,000 in coverage may seem like an adequate amount to you. But, five or ten years from now you may have children, a larger home with a steeper mortgage, automobile payments, etc. that would make $50,000 disappear very quickly in the event of your death. This is especially true if you're the major breadwinner in your home.

Discuss your life insurance options with your financial advisor, as well as your fiancé to ensure that the coverage you purchase is adequate to cover your expenses and take care of your family.

Tip - How much life insurance do your need?

Rule of thumb…

All of your debt + All of your long-term goals + All of your projected income = The amount of coverage you will need

Tip – You should decide the amount of the life insurance policy on your spouse and vice versa.

Tip – You should have disability insurance, too! What is disability insurance? Disability insurance protects an employed person in the event that they are injured and can not work anymore due to an accident or an illness. Disability insurance pays a person an income if they become disabled.

Questions to Ask Before Taking the Leap

1. Have you discussed insurance options with your fiancé?

2. Do you both own a vehicle and currently have separate coverage?

3. Does your insurance agent offer multiple car discounts?

4. Do both you and your fiancé have equal life insurance policies?

5. Is your fiancé the beneficiary of your life insurance policy; are you the beneficiary of hers or his? If not, why not?

6. Do you currently have home owners or renters insurance and will you need to increase your coverage after merging households?

7. If you're both covered under separate health insurance policies, is it more economical to merge policies or to maintain separate coverage?

8. If you have children, whose policy will cover your children?

9. Do you have an itemized list of your valuables with receipts and photos in a safe place?

10. Do you always keep proof of your medical coverage with you?

11. Do you or your fiancé have any sexually transmitted diseases? How do you know?

12. Have you or your fiancé had "his and hers" blood tests?

13. Do you know the difference between term life insurance and permanent life insurance? There are three types of permanent life insurance – whole, universal and variable. Do you understand how they work?

**Notes, thoughts, ideas,
questions and issues I want to
discuss with my love...**

Chapter Seven

Religious Matters

Marriage is three parts love and seven parts forgiveness of sins.

– Langdon Mitchell

*I*f you and your fiancé's religions are very different in terms of beliefs, philosophy, customs, traditions, etc., you may determine that there is not enough room or flexibility to negotiate an amicable future together unless one of you are willing to make a change and adopt the religion and beliefs of the other.

However, this may not always be the case. As a couple, you may decide that even with the religious differences your relationship can not only survive, but rather it can thrive. This is not an easy decision to make. You must thoroughly discuss the possible challenges you will face because of your difference in beliefs and how you will raise your children (if you choose to have them) in two different religions before you decide to marry.

Sharing the same, similar or closely related religions may be important to you. You may desire that your spouse have the same beliefs, religious background, customs and traditions as you. That's okay, too.

If your religions are similar or related in terms of beliefs, philosophy, customs, traditions, etc. then you may consider one partner switching or converting to the other's religion for the sake of unity. This can be a formal conversion or it can be informal wherein neither of you actually convert, but both of you decide to attend religious observances together.

Your involvement and your commitment level to your religion could be different, regardless of whether you share the same religion or not, and this could help you to determine which partner should adopt the other's religion, even if minimally. One partner could be very casual about attending services while the other may be extremely devoted. One of you may go to a house of worship once or twice a year to celebrate religious holidays, while the other may go to a house of worship every week and sometimes more than once a week.

In addition to having different religions and practicing them in different ways, there are people who don't necessarily believe in religion and may or may not focus on spirituality or oneness with the universe. That's okay as well provided both of you understand each other before you get married.

What's important is that you talk about and understand each other's religious backgrounds, needs, and expectations and make a commitment to respect your partner's beliefs and values before you tie the knot. Discovering or first talking about this topic after you're already married could present unnecessary challenges. Even if you assume that you both have the same religious foundations, this is a very important subject to talk about openly and honestly before you marry.

Being on the same "religious page" will be important for certain religious occasions like your wedding and the observance of religious holidays. It will also be important for many ongoing, lifelong choices you make, like how you worship and how you raise your children. However, being on the same page doesn't necessarily mean that one or the other will have to give up their beliefs. In the following pages, you'll find tips and resources to help you bridge the religious gap within your marriage.

Weekly Services

What counts in making a happy marriage is not so much how compatible you are, but how you deal with incompatibility.

– George Levinger

f both of you belong to different religions and choose to keep it that way, perhaps you'll decide to go to your respective religious observances without your partner. Or maybe you'll alternate; go to one partner's place of worship sometimes and switch to the other partner's place of worship at other times. You can work on this arrangement by trying out different variations during your courtship.

You'll also have to decide where you will get married and who will preside over your nuptials. If the type of wedding ceremony means more to spouse A than spouse B, then maybe spouse B will yield to spouse A's wishes to get married in their house of worship.

Another arrangement could be to combine, merge or blend your two types of religious ceremonies into one. This would require creativity and imagination from both of you in order to orchestrate a tasteful, meaningful wedding ceremony. Also, you would have to receive the blessings from each of your religious celebrants and ask for their advice and participation.

Families

*Mother-in-law: a woman who destroys her son-in-law's
peace of mind by giving him a piece of hers.*

– Author Unknown

You can count on your families to have an opinion on this topic. They may be gentle or subtle and simply ask questions to understand or to insure that you've thought about what you're getting into regarding different religions. They may

support you and your fiancé in whatever decision you make, just as long as the two of you are happy.

On the other end of the spectrum are families who will flat out disagree with you and your choices regarding this subject. Some people are vehemently opposed to marrying outside of their religion. You may have a member or members in your family who share these beliefs. You probably are already fully aware of anyone in your family who fits this bill. When you present your desire to get married to your family, you'll have to choose how to deal with these particular family members. You and your fiancé will have to be united, for this is the first of many tests and challenges that you and your soon-to-be-spouse will have to contend with during your life together. This can set the stage for how issues will be handled 'till death do you part.

People with dissimilar religions often find ways to merge their wedding ceremony and families into one happy home. The following is a list of resources for merged couples and families:

* http://www.interfaithfamily.com This magazine focuses on marriages between Jewish and Non-Jewish couples and discusses topics such as holiday traditions, conversions, and growing up in an interfaith family.

* http://marriage.about.com/od/interfaith/tp/interfaithbooks. htm This link contains a great listing of books for the interfaith couple to help them manage the challenges they face on a day-to-day basis.

* http://marriage.about.com/od/interfaith/a/interfacoping.htm This link has a list of do's and don'ts for the interfaith couple.

* http://islam.about.com/blinterfaith.htm This link focuses on marriages between Muslim and Non-Muslim couples and discusses topics and parameters such as holiday traditions, conversions, and rearing children in an interfaith family.

* http://marriage.about.com/od/interfaith/Interfaith_Marriages. htm This link contains information for the interfaith couple to help them navigate any additional challenges they may encounter.

Same Religion/No Religion/
Different Levels of Practicing/Morals and Beliefs

One shouldn't be too inquisitive in life
either about God's secrets or one's wife.

– Geoffrey Chaucer, The Canterbury Tales

It is obvious that marriages between two people who are of the same religion have fewer challenges, less uncertainty and fewer differences of opinion when it comes to how the family should worship than those with different religions. Nonetheless, there still could be challenges ahead.

Think about it; as you and your spouse grow, learn, live and find out who you really are in this life, your views and beliefs may change. This may include your religion. Just think of what it could do to your marriage if one of you decides to change his or her belief system. The challenges to your relationship could become immense, depending on the other half's degree of belief in their current religion.

It is my understanding that some religious affiliations believe that if one spouse leaves the religion, the other should follow suit. And if the other doesn't follow, their marriage may end in divorce. Therefore, a marriage that is grounded solidly in the fact that both partners share the same religion may not be on solid ground at all.

A marriage should be based on common goals, beliefs, and a love for your partner. If it's solely founded on the commonness of your religious beliefs, the foundation could crumble in time.

What if you and your fiancé are atheist but after marriage one of you decides to join and practice the teachings of an organized religion? Or, vice versa. Sometimes a major life event can change or alter the religious feeling one may have. Marriage, having children, winning the lottery, achieving a major goal, losing a loved one, recovering from a dependency, getting a promotion, bonus or substantial raise, being involved in a severe accident, etc. are examples where one's religious beliefs may be challenged or altered. Could you imagine your fiancé suddenly changing their religion? Could your fiancé deal with your newfound religion?

I have a friend who met her husband while attending a church. She had never been religious, grew up in an atheist home, had found religion for the first time in her life, and fell in love with a man who was in the single's group and also sang in the choir. This man was unlike any man she had ever met; he seemed to have a deep rooted belief in God, and she wanted to be like him.

After a few months of dating, the couple decided to marry. They were married in the church where they met and all of their friends, family, and fellow church members witnessed their nuptials. The sky was the limit for this young, newly married couple and everyone knew their relationship was created on solid ground within the church. Everyone thought their marriage would last.

As soon as the couple returned home from their honeymoon, things took a drastic turn for the worse. The man who was supposed to be a devout Christian and dedicated to the church no longer wanted to attend church services and furthermore, he did not allow his new bride to attend without him. He turned his back on the church the second he landed a bride and within one month, their marriage failed.

This is a drastic example of how things can go wrong, even if they seem right. Obviously the man was in the church for all the wrong reasons and was pretting to be someone he was not. But these things do happen. Most often it's not such a drastic change, but life brings on maturity and self-awareness and development and religious beliefs can change. Can your relationship withstand a religious change?

Questions to Ask Before Taking the Leap

1. Do you and your fiancé share the same religious beliefs?

2. Do you share the same morals?

3. Do you worship similarly?

4. Do you attend church together and do you both want to attend or do either of you find yourself dragging or coaxing your partner to services?

5. If your partner changes their religious beliefs, will that make a difference in your marriage?

6. If you change your religious beliefs, will your marriage still be on solid ground?

7. Do you share similar beliefs in how your children should be raised?

8. If you have different religions, have you agreed in which religion your children will be raised?

9. What are your families' beliefs about religion and will they interfere in your marriage?

10. If you or your partner has a job within a specific religion, such as ministerial or pastoral, if the other partner changes his or her religious beliefs will that make a difference in the marriage?

11. Is your engagement based solely on religion, beliefs, or morals?

12. Would you consider yourself more spiritual than religious?

Notes, thoughts, ideas, questions and issues I want to discuss with my love...

Chapter Eight

Housing Matters
(Renting or Owning)

Home is a place not only of strong affections, but of entire unreserve;
it is life's undress rehearsal, its backroom, its dressing room.

– Harriet Beecher Stowe

One of the first ways marital transitioning manifests itself is when you move into a common home and begin building a new life together.

Marriages bring on new prospects for your life, new adventures and a degree of uncertainty about your future. Merging households, lives and lifestyles is always an adventure regardless of how well or how long you've known your fiancé.

The adventure begins with things you may never have thought of while dating such as: Will you purchase or rent a house or apartment where neither of you have lived before? Are you or your fiancé moving into the other's home that's already established? Do you have the same or similar tastes in home decorating?

The subject probably came up shortly after the proposal, but you may not have discussed what it would take to merge your households – until now. The million dollar question is…Where are you going to live?

Location, location, location…

Do both of you already live in the same town? Do you plan to stay and live in the same town or city after you're married? Do you currently live in the same state or regional area? Do one or both of you live near family? Do one or both of you have children and feel the need to remain close to their school and/or support system? Does one of you or both of you have to live in close proximity to your job or business? Did you have a long distance courtship and now one of you has to make a long distance journey in order for you to be together? Are you facing the possibility of a one-time, long distance move based on a new job/career? Do you have to consider the probability of constant long distance moving due to business travel or military travel?

Have you already decided to live in one or the other's home or will both of you move into a new place of residence? Will you be renting an apartment or a house? Will you purchase a condo or a house? Will you invest in a multi-family home, living in one apartment and renting out the other(s)? Will you live with one set of parents in order to save for a down payment on your own home? Will you build your dream home? Will you build a home on the family property or farm? Questions, questions, questions…

Have you discussed these important plans? Do you know what you want? Do you know what your fiancé wants? You'll have to consider many things to answer these questions. What is your lifestyle? How were you raised? What do you like? How have you always dreamed of living? What can you afford?

As you can tell by the numerous questions, there are many, many options for newly married couples. It all comes down to where you need to live because of employment, children, support, how much you can afford, and what you're willing to spend in order to live the lifestyle you and your soon-to-be spouse want to live. For some couples where both may have been born and raised in one location, been educated and met their significant other in the same location, these questions are of foreign nature. They don't even have to think twice about where they will live. They will naturally establish a new home together practically down the road from where they grew up and lived most or all of their lives without any discussion or thought. For other couples, these questions resonate because where they will live after getting married is not quite that simple.

Even if you know where you want to live geographically, there are some things to consider.

Here are some of your options:

- Renting an apartment –
  - Pro – Little or no upkeep or maintenance.
  - Pro – Usually located in or near an urban environment, meaning close to stores, restaurants, and attractions.
  - Pro - More affordable than a traditional home (no down payment).
  - Pro – Sometimes comes with a pool, entertaining area, gym, and other amenities.
  - Pro – Organized activities given by the apartment management.
  - Pro – Added security and maintenance support.
  - Con – Some apartments won't allow their tenants to paint walls or add custom elements to the structure, unless the apartment is owned by the tenant.
  - Con – Neighbors can be noisy and too close.
  - Con – Lack of privacy.
  - Con – No control over who is in the common areas when you're entertaining.
  - Con – Some apartments do not allow pets.
- Renting a house –
  - Pro – Privacy.
  - Pro – More space.
  - Pro – Possibly rent to own.
  - Pro – Suburban instead of urban living (Could be a pro or a con depending on what you like).
  - Pro – A yard.
  - Pro – When renting, landlord takes care of maintenance.
  - Pro – Move into a home with little money up front.
  - Con – A yard - mowing.

- Con – Landlord could sell home.
- Con – No equity in home.
- Con – Some landlords do not allow pets.

  Pro – Not as expensive as a ready to move in home.
- Pro – Fix it up according to your taste.
- Pro – Gain equity from your investment/labor.
- Con – Possibility of spending more money on repairs than with a ready to move in home.
- Con – Newlyweds may have little time to fix up a home.
- Buying a condo –
  - Pro – Costs less than a traditional, single-family home.
  - Pro – Usually in urban area (again, this could be a pro or a con).
  - Pro – Very little maintenance.
  - Con – Lack of privacy.
  - Con – Association fees.
- Buying a townhouse –
  - Pro – Costs less than traditional, single-family home.
  - Pro – Usually in an urban area.
  - Pro – Very little maintenance.
  - Con – Lack of privacy.
  - Con – Association fees.
- Buying a house in the suburbs –
  - Pro – Privacy.
  - Pro – More space.
  - Pro – Suburban instead of urban living (if you like living in the suburbs).
  - Pro – A yard.
  - Pro – Minimal traffic (debatable).
  - Con – A yard - mowing.

- ✦ Con – Maintenance and upkeep.
- ✦ Con – No equity in home (this depends on your down payment and the negotiated sale price versus the market value of the house. Your equity in your home could take time to build).
- ✦ Con – Commute.
- ✤ Buying a condo in a high rise in the big city –
  - ✦ Pro – Little or no upkeep or maintenance.
  - ✦ Pro – Close to stores, restaurants, and attractions.
  - ✦ Pro – Usually comes with a pool, entertaining area, gym, or other amenities.
  - ✦ Pro – Organized activities given by the apartment management.
  - ✦ Pro – Added security and maintenance support.
  - ✦ Con – Some apartments won't allow their tenants to paint walls or add custom elements to the structure, unless the apartment is owned by the tenant.
  - ✦ Con – Neighbors can be noisy and too close.
  - ✦ Con – Lack of privacy.
  - ✦ Con – No control over who is in the common areas when you're entertaining.
  - ✦ Con – City noise.
  - ✦ Con – More costly than the suburbs.
- ✤ Buying a quaint home in the country –
  - ✦ Pro – Privacy.
  - ✦ Pro – Space.
  - ✦ Pro – Farm or garden.
  - ✦ Pro – Quiet.
  - ✦ Pro – A yard.
  - ✦ Pro – Costs less than urban or suburban living.
  - ✦ Pro – Equity.
  - ✦ Con – A yard - mowing.

- Con – Commute.
- Con – Longer drive to attractions.

* Buying and running a farm –
  - Pro – Privacy.
  - Pro – Space.
  - Pro – Animals and garden.
  - Pro – Quiet.

  - Pro – A yard.
  - Pro – Costs less than urban or suburban living.
  - Pro – Equity.
  - Pro/Con? – Mowing, plowing, milking, feeding, planting, harvesting, etc. (this could be a pro or a con).
  - Con – Physically challenging.
  - Con – Commute.
  - Con – Longer drive to attractions.

* Buying and living in a multi-family home, while renting out the other units –
  - Pro – Make an income from your investment.
  - Pro – Equity.

- ✦ Con – Lack of privacy.
- ✦ Con – Maintenance and upkeep.
- ✦ Con – Dealing with tenants, collecting rent, and possible evictions.

- ✦ Living at your parent's home while saving up enough to buy your own place –
  - ✦ Pro – No upkeep or maintenance.
  - ✦ Pro - Affordable.
  - ✦ Pro – Save money for own home.
  - ✦ Pro – Close to family.
  - ✦ Con – Close to family.
  - ✦ Con – No privacy.
  - ✦ Con – *No privacy!*
  - ✦ Con – Less opportunity to get to know each other. Plenty of unwanted or unsolicited advice.
  - ✦ Con – No control over who is in the common areas when you're entertaining.

No matter which option you choose – apartment, condo, or house, "home is where the heart is" and newlywed couples can make any dwelling into a home.

With the housing market the way it is today, and investors creating an income from purchasing foreclosures and fixer uppers to "flip" for a profit, some young couples are finding it more difficult to buy/rent their first home in the same neighborhood they grew up or work. Commuting is becoming more commonplace as the further out you move, the lower the price.

There is a lack of decent, affordable housing in this country, and newlyweds are one of the biggest groups in our population who are affected by the housing shortage. It makes you wonder if our children or grandchildren will be able to afford to purchase their own home.

Consult with your realtor, banker, or financial planner to help you determine which housing options will best suit your needs.

To Own or Rent

I told my mother-in-law that my house was her house,
and she said, "Get the hell off my property."

– Joan Rivers

It's easy to say that owning a home is the best thing you can do. In most cases, it's better to pay your own mortgage, building equity and wealth, than to pay your landlord's mortgage.

However, there are other factors to consider. How is the housing market? If interest rates are prohibitively high, you may find that it's too expensive to purchase at that moment and you may decide to wait for a few months or years until the market swings in the other direction. Or, perhaps you or your fiancé has a job that involves travel or relocating, and you're more than certain that you'll be moving in a relatively short period of time. Purchasing a home and then having to sell it soon thereafter may cause more headaches than just renting for a while longer until you can settle down.

Except for these types of circumstances, owning a home is usually the best option. Many times, the difference between homeowners and renters is the ability to afford the down payment for a home. After the down payment and closing costs are paid, the amounts for monthly rent vs. monthly mortgage payments are very similar. If neither of you has saved enough for the down payment of a home, then now is a great time to start! If this is important to you, you'll need to make wise choices, hard choices that will enable you to achieve your goal of homeownership.

If you read this before you get married – GREAT! What you are about to read may change your life.

The average cost of a wedding, or more specifically, a reception in the United States is more than $25,000. Some say that the average is approaching $40,000.

If you have the means to pay this amount of money for your reception and you already own a home, although it's an expensive party, you can afford it.

I know a couple who was about to be married. I was talking to the father of the bride at a function and he shared with me that his wife and his daughter were going to drive him straight to the crazy house. They wanted everything to be perfect for the upcoming wedding. Their daughter was always treated like a princess and this wedding would be fit for, well, a princess. He confided in me that the wedding was going to cost in excess of $75,000 and he was paying for it!

But most couples take on this huge expenditure when sadly, they can't really afford it. They do this for several reasons, including: it's expected of them, they have always dreamed of having a big wedding, they have loads of family and friends who wouldn't understand it if they weren't invited to their wedding, etc.

Don't feel pressured to spend $25,000, $40,000, or more for a wedding reception when that money could be put to better use. Yes, I said it! That amount of money is quite sizable, and could be spent on something far more substantial than your wedding reception.

I call a wedding reception a four-hour party. After you break it down, that's really all it is. I'm not saying that it won't be the most memorable four-hour party you'll ever throw, but let's be realistic; it's a four hour party!

Let's say your other consideration is to purchase a starter home for $120,000. The $25,000 to $30,000 you were planning to spend on your four-hour party could easily be the down payment and closing costs for your new home that will serve you for many, many years. Or stated differently, your new home that will serve you much, much longer than four hours!

Here's an idea. After you've purchased your new home, have your reception by throwing a party at your house! You'll spend a fraction of what it would cost to have a traditional reception held at a beautiful country club; plus it will be far more meaningful and very wise. You won't even have to limit it to four hours!

You'll never read this in a bride's magazine. You'll never hear that from your wedding consultant (I'm guessing – I can truthfully say that *I've* never seen an article in a bride's magazine or heard a wedding consultant suggest this…). Why would you? Why would they ever say anything like that? The wedding industry is a multi-billion dollar industry, and it's still growing. They say they have your best interests in mind – to make sure you have the best wedding possible. I'm sure that's true, but let's get real! They're in the wedding business for a reason – to make money. How are they going to bring in the big bucks by talking their clients into saving for their marriage, versus spending money on their wedding? I'm not saying their point of view is a bad thing; after all, they're in business to make a profit. And if you can afford a big wedding, or your parents are paying and a big wedding is what they want for you, let the good times roll! But if the cost of your wedding is the difference in you being able to own a home or rent, I say think very carefully about it. Do you get my point?

In the previous housing options I listed the pros and cons of owning, renting, apartments, houses and condos. Let's take a look once more at the differences between owning and renting:

- Own -
    - Pro – Privacy.
    - Pro – Space.
    - Pro – Possibly suburban instead of urban living.
    - Pro – A yard.
    - Pro – Equity.
    - Pro – Decorate to your taste.
    - Con – A yard - mowing.
    - Con – Down payment.
    - Con – Maintenance and upkeep.
    - Con – Commute.
- Rent –
    - Pro – Affordable.
    - Pro – No maintenance or upkeep.
    - Pro – Possibly no yard.
    - Con – No equity.
    - Con – Lack of privacy.
    - Con – White walls – meaning bland décor or lack of your personality.

The following is a list of tools that can help you decide where to live, and whether you should rent or own:

✦ Calculator to help you determine the best decision for your family. http://www.homes.com/Content/Calculators/index.cfm?Page=RentOrBuy&ID=3_53

✦ Making an educated choice about the decision that is best for you. http://www.relo.com/consumer/planningmove/firstTimeHomeOwners/RentOrBuy.aspx

✦ Canadian mortgage calculator helps determine which is best for Canadian families. http://www.canadianmortgagecalculators.net/rentbuy.html

✦ Relocation Calculator helps you decide if you and/or your spouse should relocate. http://salarycenter.monster.com/articles/relocate/spouse

Long-Distance Marriages

How lucky I am to have something that makes saying goodbye so hard.

– From the movie Annie

$\mathcal{D}$id you have a long distance courtship or will your marriage be one in which you will have to live apart from each other? There are challenges that you'll face because of the physical and geographical distance in your relationship.

Let's keep it real; your marriage and communication will have to be very strong and understanding to withstand the temptations that come along with being away from your spouse for elongated periods of time.

You may be marrying a person that travels for work. Intellectually, you may realize that your fiancé travels and you know you'll have to deal with the distance between you, but that first business trip, followed by subsequent ones, may still be very difficult to experience. This is not only difficult for the person staying home while their partner goes away. It may be just as hard, or sometimes harder, for the one doing the traveling. It's challenging to be the one who is pulled and yanked away from your home and family. Traveling may have been okay, or even fun and glamorous when you were single. But now that you're married, that routine trip may feel like a dreaded reality that is way too unfair and difficult to endure.

If you or your spouse is a member of the military reserves, or you get a job promotion, time spent away from your partner may be something you didn't even consider when you were dating, engaged, or subsequent to your marriage. Traveling and being apart from each other may be a totally new phenomenon for you. But unfortunately, it sometimes comes with the territory.

On the other hand, some couples feel that their marriage has endured the test of time because one or both of them travels so much! These couples feel that if they were constantly together all of the time they might end up hurting each other! They feel that being apart enhances their relationship in ways that most of us don't understand. They also feel that the quality of their time together is extra special, perhaps even more special than it would be if they were always together.

Whether you are separated often due to military or business travel, or because one partner spends their weekdays in the city to save on the commute; the following are a few tips to ensure that the physical distance in your relationship does not become an emotional distance as well.

- Communicate! – I know I've mentioned communication in several areas of this book. But really, communication is the main ingredient in a healthy, happy marriage. So, communicate your feelings about the physical distance. Be careful to state your concerns without accusing your partner of any wrongdoing. And respond to your partner's concerns without becoming defensive.

- Realize that the distance is only for a certain period of time and it's not forever. Work together to make the separation as painless as possible.

- Maintain your commitment to your partner. Even though you're physically separated, go through your day as if your spouse were present. (When the cat's away, this mouse won't play!) Stay committed.

- Trust your spouse and don't give them a reason to distrust you.

- Do special things when you're together to keep your marriage fresh and alive.

- Stay in touch daily. The Internet is a great way to catch up on the happenings of your day without spending money on long distance calls or cell phone minutes. Most hotels have free Internet access. If you have a cell phone plan or family plan where your spouse can be called for free, take advantage of the plan. Spend at least an hour each day discussing things that you would normally talk about at home. If it's not free and it costs money to communicate, spend the money and communicate! Do whatever it takes!

- Be honest with each other. If you have concerns, doubts or fears, tell your partner. He or she may share your concerns. Discuss what's troubling you and work together to find a solution for your concerns.

- When it's possible, travel together. There are some trips that can be made as a couple; take advantage of those and if you're the one always on the road, invite your partner along.

✦ When the traveling partner returns, don't greet him or her with a mile long "honey-do list" (a list of tasks for you to do, prepared by your honey!). Relax! Spend time together and catch up on things before you bring up what went wrong, what needs to be fixed, how you haven't had a decent meal in a week or any other negative, energy draining topics. It can wait!

Here are some resources for families who struggle because of business and military travel:

✦ http://www.longdistancerelationships.net/faqs.htm   Military Travel, Online Newspaper column for military couples

✦ http://marriage.about.com/gi/dynamic/offsite.htm?zi=1/XJ/Ya&sdn=marriage&cdn=people&tm=4&gps=111_1_936_506&f=11&su=p689.109.140.ip_&tt=14&bt=1&bts=1&zu=http%3A//www.plaintec.net/page5.html

✦ Army Morale, Welfare and Recreation www.ArmyMWR.com

✦ http://www.myarmylife-too.com/skins/malt/home.aspx?AllowSSL=true

✦ Navy Resource www.life-lines2000.org

✦ Navy's Morale, Welfare and Recreation http://www.mwr.navy.mil

✦ For marriages where both spouses are members of the military - Getting assigned to the same duty station. http://marriage.about.com/cs/militarymarriages/a/join-spouse.htm

- Returning home - Planning homecoming celebrations http://marriage.about.com/cs/militarymarriages/qt/homecoming.htm

- General information with many links for and about military spouses http://www.usatoday.com/news/washington/2006-02-04-army-spouse_x.htm

- Ready to move but your spouse isn't? Support services for the spouse who relocates. http://www.morsemoving.com/spouse.html

Questions to Ask Before Taking the Leap

1. Do you live in the same town already?

2. Do you plan to stay and live in the same town or city after you're married?

3. Do you live in the same state or regional area?

4. Do one or both of you live near family?

5. Do one or both of you have children and need to remain close to their school and/or support system?

6. Does one or both of you have to live in close proximity to your job or business?

7. Did you have a long distance courtship and now one of you has to make a long distance journey in order for you to be together? Or, do both of you have to consider a long distance move based on a new job/career, business or military travel?

8. Have you already decided to live in one or the other's home or will both of you move into a new place of residence?

9. Will you rent an apartment or a house?

10. Will you purchase a condo or a house?

11. Will you invest in a multi-family home, living in one apartment and renting out the other(s)?

12. Will you live with one set of parents in order to save for a down payment on your own home?

13. Will you build your dream home?

14. Will you build a home on the family property?

15. Have you discussed these important plans?

16. Do you know what you want and do you know what your fiancé wants?

17. How have you always dreamed of living?

18. What can you afford?

19. Would you consider changing your job or career in order to avoid having to travel now that you're getting married?

20. Would you be willing to take a cut in pay in a new job that did not require travel?

Notes, thoughts, ideas, questions and issues I want to discuss with my love...

Chapter Nine

Day-to-Day Living

Strike an average between what a woman thinks of her husband a month before she marries him and what she thinks of him a year afterward, and you will have the truth about him.

– H.L. Mencken, A Book of Burlesques, 1916

*A*s your lives merge into one, you'll develop your own routines, schedules, rituals, and practices. Some of them will be based on rituals that each of your families shared. Others will evolve from your interaction and chemistry (synergy) together. They may even develop from dreams that you've always had – "When I'm married with my own family, I'd love to…"

Are your lifestyles compatible? Is one of you the "early bird" and the other a "night owl?" Is one of you a homebody whereas the other is a party animal? Is one of you the type who likes a million gadgets, toys, bells, and whistles while the other is quite comfortable with the bare minimum? Oh, you're going to have a ball! In this new adventure you're going to discover all of the things about your partner that you did not, could not or chose not to see while you were dating. There may be annoying habits that you'll discover for the first time once you're married. Things that didn't bother you before the "I do's" may become annoying once you move in together. This is perfectly normal!

The key to working out the new challenges in your relationship will be to communicate with each other so that you can find ways in which both of you can be happy. You'll have to learn how to accept things about your partner that you don't necessarily love. But that's okay! Your partner will have to accept things about you that he or she doesn't necessarily love either. You'll learn to share disapproval in a thoughtful, caring way and you'll learn to hear criticisms about you or your habits without reacting defensively.

When you're dating, even after you've dated for quite a considerable amount of time, you and your fiancé may naturally put your best foot forward. A dating environment is different than an environment where you live with each other from day to day as a married couple. When your fiancé comes over for a visit, regardless of how close you are, there's a host/visitor relationship. In other words, you clearly live there while your fiancé is a guest. You have all of your belongings there and you've set up an environment where it's comfortable for you and you feel "at home."

Your fiancé, the guest, even if he or she is very, very comfortable and "feels as though your place is a second home," is still not at home until their "stuff" has been moved and there is no longer another home that is used as his or her primary dwelling.

You'll have to learn the dance of maintaining your "self" while simultaneously sharing your "space" and developing a new life as a married couple, a new unit, and a new entity.

Merging Households

Soul-mates are people who bring out the best in you.
They are not perfect, but are always perfect for you.

– Author Unknown

After you've decided where you're going to live once you're married, you now have to face the task of merging households. What does that mean? It's a wide category that includes loads of factors and variables. But mostly it can be described by the following:

Where did you live before?

Regardless of where you were living before the wedding, whether you were living at home with your parents, in your own apartment, house, perhaps in a dorm, with roommates, in military barracks, or even if you were already rooming with your fiancé, oftentimes there will be some kind of transition in living arrangements after you marry. Sometimes this is a minor transition, but most times it's major.

The transition of your living arrangements and the operations of each of your households before you were married compared to the living arrangements and the operations of your combined households after you are married is what I mean when I say "merging households."

It will take a lot of patience, understanding, and the willingness to be flexible. For this transition to be smooth, both of you may very well likely have to be open to negotiation; sometimes letting go of things that used to be important to you. If all of this is done with the goal of living together in a place that both of you are comfortable and can call "home," then this transition period will work out for the better.

On the other hand, if one of you is stubborn or unwilling to listen to the needs of your partner, or has a strong bond to material things or particular habits, customs, practices, or rituals, then this transition period has the potential to be both unrewarding and very stressful. If both of you are stubborn that will surely make this situation even worse.

Let's take the scenario where each of you own or rent your own apartment or home. And let's say you decide that you'll live together in one of those homes after you're married and you'll sell or give up the lease and move out of the other. This may be an extremely difficult situation. The scenarios wherein both of you will be moving into a new home; a home where neither of you have lived prior to getting married, may be a little easier for a couple of reasons. The first is that neither of you have any more of an attachment to the new place than the other. You'll be starting anew. You can build your new home together on equal footing.

Also, when you move into your new home, you'll merely move the belongings you want into the new house. There won't be any pre-existing articles that you'll have to decide to move out if the partner moving in doesn't care for them, or if you're short on space.

But even this scenario has challenges. You'll have to coordinate when each of your respective leases are up (or your closing dates) with the date you're able to move into your new home. Some furniture and personal items will come from one of your homes, while other furniture and more personal items will come from the other and perhaps additional furniture and/or appliances will be delivered brand new. If your lease expires or your closing date is the same day that you've been told your new home will be ready, that may be cutting it too close.

For instance, what if there is a problem with your new home and your move-in date gets delayed a week? Or what if it's raining cats and dogs on the day that you were planning to move? You can give yourself some additional time and flexibility by overlapping the date you have to be out of your existing home with the move in date of your new home.

If you're due to move into your new home on June 1st, you may schedule the day you have to be out of your existing home for July 1st or June 14th. It may seem senseless to pay for two or three homes simultaneously, but in the event of an unforeseen delay, it could be a life saver and you'll be so glad you planned ahead!

You'll also need a plan for the items that you had in your respective homes prior to getting married that you will not be moving into your new home. Some things you may want to keep in the family and therefore they'll go to relatives, while others can be donated or sold. Having a plan for these things before your moving day will alleviate some of the stress of having to part with treasured possessions.

Okay, back to the scenario of you both moving into a home where one partner already lived before getting married. One thing you'll have to be mindful of is you want to ensure that you both feel comfortable in your marital home. You wouldn't want the person who's moving in to feel uncomfortable in his or her new home. You wouldn't want the person moving in to continue to feel like a guest. You wouldn't want all of the furniture, decorations, entertainment center, photos, utensils, and accessories to belong to the person who already lived there, while the person who moved in only has clothing and personal items to call their own.

Thus, the person who already resides in the place must be willing to get rid of some belongings, to make space, if you will, for the other's belongings.

This can be done in a logical, sensible way. For instance, let's say you each have a bedroom set. One bedroom set is a relatively new queen sized bed with matching furniture, while the other is a twin sized bed with a dresser from college days that has one drawer missing and a couple of other old, damaged, unmatched pieces making up the "set." Well, you may jointly decide to keep the queen sized bed and matching furniture and take the opportunity to get rid of the other "bedroom set."

Similarly, if you have a dining room in your new home and only one of you has a dining room set, you may want to keep that dining room set.

In these cases it seems logical to keep the queen sized bed set as well as the sole dining room set.

Wouldn't that be lovely?

Sometimes it isn't always as simple as it appears. What if the queen sized bed and matching furniture is pink and white with flowers and lace? What if it was made of dark wood and was very masculine? What if the dining room set was solid oak, but your partner always dreamed of a mahogany dining room set or one featuring an avant-garde, beveled glass table top? Or what if the dining room set was very informal, but your partner always wanted a formal dining room – or vise versa. What if your partner's queen sized bedroom set still had notches, either literally or figuratively, which reminded either or both of you of all the sexual conquests your partner had prior to getting married?

This is not a purely logical decision, is it? You'll have to balance logic and emotion in your decisions regarding merging households. On some issues or decisions, logic will prevail. On others, you may have to be willing to trust your emotional instincts and come to a mutual decision. This might mean that even though each of you had a bedroom set, you may choose to save for a new one that's a style you both like. Or, you could decide that you'll keep and use one of the bedroom sets for a year or two while you budget and save for a new one in the near future.

Be realistic about your short-term plans. If you plan and budget to get new furniture in the first year or two and you're also planning to start a family, you may find yourself borrowing heavily from your furniture coffer to finance the needs of your new addition to your family.

Whatever you decide, the important thing to remember is to be honest and voice your opinions and feelings to your partner up front. Don't wait until moving day to say, "I HATE THAT BEDROOM SET! If that bedroom set enters my house, I'm sleeping in another room, or at my mother's house!" That would be inappropriate and unfair, to say the least.

If you have any concerns or issues about anything regarding furniture, furnishings and accessories, you must be open, honest, courteous, and empathetic when discussing it with your partner. The earlier you discuss your feelings, the better.

If the combination of furniture from your individual households will be too much when you merge into one, you may have to get rid of some furniture and other kitchen and household items. You can donate the items that you won't need to a local charitable organization. Save your receipts; the IRS is tightening the reins on tax laws but you still may be able to write off all or some of your contributions on your annual income tax return. Or, you may want to hold a garage sale and use the proceeds to purchase household items that you need. You could even use the proceeds to open a joint savings account.

Although the task of merging households may seem daunting, as long as you communicate your feelings and are considerate of your partner's feelings, you should be able to work through any roadblock(s).

Chores

Assumptions are the termites of relationships.

– Henry Winkler

There are a multitude of chores necessary to maintain a household. Some need to be done with different regularity. Some are daily chores. Some are performed at weekly intervals. Some are seasonal. Some chores are done in the home, and others are outdoor chores or automotive maintenance "chores."

Who is going to do all of these chores once you're married? If you have lived in separate homes before your wedding, these chores are done or handled by each of you respectively. But after your wedding day, when you're living together, who gets to do what?

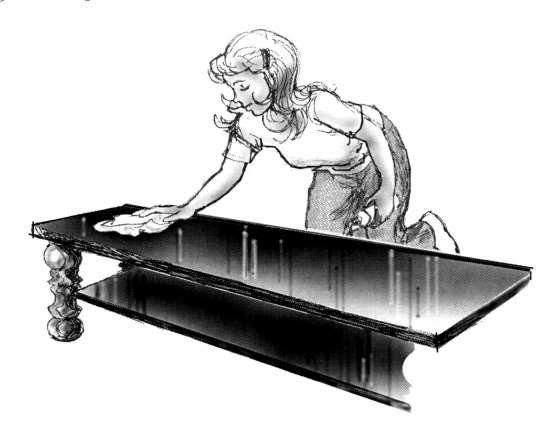

To help you decide the division of labor, answering these questions may help:

* Will both of you work outside of the home?

* What are your ideas or beliefs of who does what in the household?

* Did you grow up in a household where your parents divided chores based on "traditional" male and female roles? Do both of you support that now?

* Did you grow up in a household where your parents divided up household chores based on a "progressive" model? Do both of you support that now?

It doesn't really matter which model you adopt. What matters is that you are both on the same page.

Problems can arise when one of you believes one way is the "right" way to handle chores, and the other believes a different way is the "right" way. You'll have to come to a compromise or an understanding of how you'll run your household. It may be based on models learned when you were growing up in your respective households or it may be based on a new model that you develop together.

Being open and flexible will help tremendously in this area. Everything doesn't have to be done "your" way. Just as there is more than one way to skin a cat, there is more than one way to wash the dishes, and there is more than one cleaning product that effectively cleans the shower/tub. I know couples who have fought about the position of the toilet paper roll! This occurs when one partner strongly believes the toilet paper roll should be "overhand" where the roll spins away from the wall, towards the user. While the other partner insists the best way is when the toilet paper roll is positioned "underhand" where the roll spins towards the wall. There may be different solutions to any dilemma and just because your mate does something different than what you are accustomed to doesn't mean they're wrong.

Perhaps listing all of the chores that have to be done and assigning the one who'll be responsible for each item will help. Maybe you'll both just pitch in whenever something is needed without the need for hard and fast "rules." Or maybe you'll decide to do chores together.

Whatever you decide at first, your list may have to be revised or adjusted for better efficiency, or perhaps to accommodate a new job or position which alters your work hours and affects your time at home to do certain chores.

Here are just a few of the typical chores of a household:

Indoor chores, not limited to…

Cooking

Setting the table

Washing dishes / loading dishwasher

Cleaning the kitchen

Cleaning the bathrooms

Changing sheets

Cleaning the bedrooms

Cleaning the living room / dining room / other rooms

Dusting

Sweeping

Vacuuming

Mopping

Washing clothes at home or going to the Laundromat

Folding clothes

Ironing

Taking and picking up the dry cleaning

Watering flowers and plants

Emptying the garbage

Grocery shopping

Feeding pets

Bringing in the mail

Spring cleaning

Storing the winter clothes / storing the spring and summer clothes

Picking up toys / Changing diapers / Doing homework and all of the chores related to caring for children

<u>Outdoor chores, not limited to…</u>

Washing cars

Cutting the lawn

Raking leaves

Shoveling snow

Gardening

Weeding

Changing the oil in the cars

Light painting

Light repair and up keep

You may decide to hire a person to do certain chores. For instance, maybe your work schedules are so hectic that you may decide to hire a house cleaner to do major housework on a periodic basis. Or, you may not have the tools or the proper receptacles to discard engine oil, so you take your car to a quick oil change service instead of changing it yourselves.

If you eat out a lot, that will reduce the need to cook on a daily basis. But paying for all of these services can be costly. You'll have to weigh whether it's worth it or not. By doing these chores yourself, you'll be able to save more and / or free up funds for other required expenses. Paying for someone else to do your chores should only be considered if you can truly afford it.

Who's Responsible for Doing What?

I'm not going to vacuum until Sears makes one you can ride on.

– Roseanne Barr

Who is responsible for doing which chores? Who is responsible for doing the work necessary to maintain your household?

There is a certain population of married couples where the husband has a full-time job and the wife does not work outside of the home. The majority of couples in this situation agree that the wife does most of the housework. They agree that the wife's work takes place within the home.

The wife then becomes responsible for managing the bulk of the household chores, and if the couple has any children, she is also the primary child care provider. For many people, this is the "traditional" arrangement for a married couple. That is based on the way things were a few decades ago, when it was not as common to have both the husband and the wife work outside the home. This was due to many factors, including the developmental stage of our society and the fact that there was less of a need for a double income in order to maintain what we called a "normal standard of living."

Today, there are a relatively few marriages where the wife works outside the home and the husband does not. Most couples in this situation agree, similarly, that since the husband is home, he should be responsible for doing the majority of the housework. This would be considered "role reversal," because the traditional gender roles are reversed.

In both of these cases, the spouse that works outside the home is labeled "the breadwinner" and the one who stays home to work is called "the homemaker." Being the homemaker is a large responsibility that is often undervalued. It's a heavy load, yet the rewards are not measured the same as working outside the home. There is no pay check, there are no promotions, and there are no bonuses. It requires a huge commitment, and it demands a variety of skills. It's a very important job, yet it is often thankless and it is never-ending. Recent studies conclude that if you were to add the value of all the individual jobs performed by housewives (or Mr. Mom), the aggregate position of "homemaker" would command a salary in excess of $100,000 per year.

Even though the homemaker stays home and does household chores every day, there is no reason why the one who works outside the home can't help out and pitch in to do their share of work around the house.

Although it may not be reasonable to expect the one who works outside the home to do 50% of the housework, that partner still lives at home; therefore, he or she should certainly be responsible for some of the housework. That would take a little of the pressure off of the person who works inside the home and it would also show appreciation and support of the unfairly thankless job of a homemaker.

Of course, the homemaker may have a proven system of doing things around the house. So, some coordination may be necessary for the other partner who's helping out. If the homemaker feels the chores that the breadwinner does in an attempt to help out have to be redone, then you're both wasting time and nothing has been gained. However, if the breadwinner has certain tasks that supplement the work of the homemaker, then that effort will be greatly appreciated.

Now comes the hard part…

There is another part of the married population where both partners work outside the home. Nowadays, this probably represents the largest percentage of married couples. Now, who is responsible for doing the household chores?

When women started working outside the home in increasing numbers, the housework was still traditionally seen as the responsibility of the woman. That meant that women ultimately ended up having two "full-time" jobs; one outside the home, and the other within the home. In an untraditional way, women were increasingly working in full-time positions and careers, while at the same time, in a traditional sense, they had the primary responsibility of doing all or most of the housework and child rearing.

At first, women claimed to be able to have it all. They were termed "super-women," and they felt that they could, and should be able to handle the demands of maintaining a full-time career outside the home while also maintaining the tremendous required household responsibilities. It didn't take long before women felt overwhelmed, unfulfilled, and unappreciated. Not to mention the effects of being overworked and stressed out began permeating women's health issues, in general.

What are the possible options for handling the housework?

- The wife does all or most of the housework.
- The husband does all or most of the housework.
- Both the wife and the husband share in the housework.
- The housework is done by hired personnel.
- Nobody does any housework and the housework doesn't get done.

Before you get married, you will each have preconceived notions of how the housework will get done – whether it's conscious or subconscious. Discussing this issue before you get married will help you understand whether you're on the same page or not. If you are on the same page - if you share the same ideas and feelings of how the household will be maintained - it's great to know that ahead of time. You won't have to make any adjustments in this area or perhaps only minor adjustments will be necessary.

If you each have a different idea of how the housework will be handled, then it's great that you've discovered this difference early. Thus, you have some time to further discuss this issue, such that you have the opportunity to come to an agreement, or at least an understanding, before you get married.

At least there will be no surprises in this area. That is the point of much of what is contained in this book. To discuss as many things as possible related to living as a married couple, before the wedding day, in an effort to build understanding toward one another, and each of you individually. It's far better to identify the areas in which you agree and also the areas in which you don't agree, such that you can communicate and creatively work on the areas where there is disagreement.

There is no "right way" or "wrong way" for each couple to handle the responsibilities of housework (Well, maybe the option listed above – The housework does not get done – that probably won't work for anyone!). What works for one couple may not necessarily work for another couple, and vise versa. What's important is that you, as a couple, should come to an agreement that truly takes into account each other's needs.

If you choose to divide the responsibilities, how do you do that?

I want to stay away from the notion and the term "50 – 50." It might be nice in a perfect world for your relationship to be "50 – 50," but it's an unrealistic goal, which, when you think about it, is very limited and has lots of room for failure.

The idea of "50 – 50" is something you strive to achieve in the big picture, but it may or may not actually occur in each component making up the big picture.

There will be some household chores that, quite frankly, one of you may be well-suited for while the other is simply not able or qualified to do. For instance, if one of you loves to cook and is a great chef, and the other can't make toast, well it just makes perfect sense and is quite obvious as to who will be doing the cooking. Now, this is cool as long as the chef in the relationship is okay with cooking all of the time.

However, be careful. While it may be fun to cook sometimes, when it becomes required that you do all of the cooking, every day, it may lose some of its charm. In this case, perhaps it would be good to give the "chef" a break once in a while. Maybe you'll agree to go out to eat periodically. Take-out food is another option. Plus, there are so many types of prepared foods that you can purchase and simply heat up.

Or, maybe the "non-chef" in the relationship can learn to read recipes and create moderately simple dishes from time to time to take some of the cooking responsibilities and again, give the chef a break. The "chef" would probably be thrilled that their partner cares enough about them to go out of their way to learn how to prepare some dishes. It would also be great if the "chef" in this relationship were very supportive of their partner who is trying their best to cook. You wouldn't want to laugh at the one trying to negotiate their way around the kitchen for what may be the first time in their life. You would also have to resist the urge to take over for them all of the time. They'll never learn to cook if you end up cooking for them. You weren't born a chef – let them make their mistakes as they learn. If a meal turns out absolutely too dreadful to eat, laugh about it together! (Remember, if only one of you is laughing, it's not funny!) Then order out for the evening!

Also, if one of you is the "designated chef," perhaps the other could be responsible for doing all of the clean-up chores in the kitchen, like washing all of the dishes, scrubbing all of the pots and pans, wiping down the stove, cleaning the oven, sweeping and mopping the kitchen floor, etc.

Each household chore that you can identify can be listed and the person who will have primary responsibility should be written next to it. Go through the list the first time and write the obvious choices or the "no brainers." There will probably be many chores that, after the first pass, won't have a name written next to it. That's okay. Go through the list again and again while discussing the pros and cons of one or the other, taking responsibility for each chore until each item on the list has someone who agrees to be the primary person responsible.

Creativity is the key here in finding different ways to support each other and find solutions to dilemmas.

Eat In or Out

The Rose Bowl is the only bowl I've ever seen that I didn't have to clean.

– Erma Bombeck

Eating out used to be a luxury. Something enjoyed once or twice a month, or reserved for special occasions. But lately, with the advent of women working outside the home and simply feeling like they don't have the time to cook nightly meals, eating out has become more and more popular as an everyday occurrence.

Men traditionally didn't even know how to cook. Now many, many women would say that they, too, don't know how to cook.

I once lived next door to an elementary school teacher who asked her class to record what they ate for a week during introductory studies on nutrition. She told me that she was expecting to see eggs and toast or cereals listed for breakfast, perhaps sandwiches and chips or burgers and fries for lunch, and beef and potatoes or chicken and pasta for dinner. But this is an example of what the children listed…

- Monday: McDonald's® for breakfast, Burger King® for lunch, Pizza Hut® for dinner

- Tuesday: Sonic® for breakfast, Wendy's® for lunch, KFC for dinner

- Wednesday: Krispy Kreme® for breakfast, What-a-Burger® for lunch, Arby's® for dinner

- Thursday: Jack-In-The-Box® for breakfast, Subway® for lunch, Taco Bell® for dinner

- Friday: 7-Eleven® for breakfast, Domino's Pizza® for lunch, Chick-fil-A® for dinner

She and all of her fellow teachers were stunned! (And frankly, so was I!)

Eating out is fun and each of us have been to and enjoyed eating at most, if not all of these restaurants. But, just like anything else, perhaps it is best enjoyed in moderation. Furthermore, there are significant health benefits to cooking and eating at home, and there are significant economic reasons too. And it has been said that the family that dines together stays together. Sitting down at the dinner table and enjoying conversation is a simple way to keep a family very close and connected.

Cooking doesn't mean you have to prepare meals suitable for gourmet chefs. These days there are so many good food choices that are partially prepared for you which make "cooking" easier than ever. Or you can follow the motto, "If you can read, you can cook."

There are dozens of cookbooks on the market that boast great, freshly prepared meals in a very little amount of time. You can even get an endless number of recipes via the Internet. Experiment and cook together!

Two-Income Family –
Does the Wife Still Get to Do All of the Housework?

I think housework is the reason most women go to the office.

– Heloise Cruse

There is no right or wrong in this scenario. What's right for one family may not work for another. Some wives enjoy going home after a day at the office and preparing dinner for their family. They may also look forward to cleaning day and being able to spend hours at home getting caught up on the chores.

But obviously, for some wives, doing housework on their day off or spending time over a hot stove after a long day at the office is not their idea of the "American dream."

I'd say that individual couples have to make a decision on what fits their lifestyle, desires, and budget. If their household is a two-income household and they can afford to pay for someone to clean it for them, it might be well worth the expenditure.

Some couples make a deal that the wife will do the inside work, while the husband takes care of the outside. But if you live in an apartment or condo, those terms may not apply because you are not responsible for outside maintenance. So, communicate and decide what's right for your income and your lifestyle. And for the guys, don't assume that your wife will automatically take care of the home. She may have a totally different perspective of what married life will be

Paying Bills

*The safe way to double your money is to fold it over once
and put it in your pocket.*

– Frank Hubbard

It's very important to establish a firm routine for paying bills. One of the best ways to "save" money over the course of many years is to pay your bills on time, all the time. Think about it – every time a bill is paid late and there is an additional charge, whether they call it a service charge or a late payment charge, that's funds out of your pocket into their pockets. That is an absolute, unnecessary waste.

Another way to look at it is: the item you purchased or the service that you used cost you a certain amount of money. And, you agreed to pay that amount for that product or service. What if that same product or service cost, say $25 more? Would you have agreed to pay for it at the higher price? Well, if you pay your bills late, that is effectively what you've done. You're now paying more for that item than you agreed to pay.

Another way to look at it is consider how well you like your credit card company. Do you like them enough to give them a tip – like the tip you'd give a waiter or waitress in a restaurant? Well, if you pay your bills routinely late and are regularly charged a service charge – you must really love them. In effect, you are tipping them each and every month. They love you! That's for sure!!!

Some people pay their bills as soon as they receive them in the mail. That's a great practice and it absolutely insures that every bill will be paid on time. They simply train themselves to write out the bills they receive, on the same day they receive it, as soon as they arrive home from work, or as a part of their ritual when arriving home from a days work or retiring for the evening.

Some people choose to save or store up their bills to pay on a periodic basis. Perhaps their routine is to "do the bills" every Saturday morning over a cup of coffee. Or, perhaps they get paid every Friday, so they choose to pay their bills based on their pay schedule.

Many people still pay their bills by writing a check and mailing in their payment. Many others have their bill payments automatically withdrawn from their checking accounts so they don't even have to physically do anything in order for their bills to get paid. This option is great, if you can do it. The entity that you owe has to offer this service. You'll need a checking account and you'd have to be certain that there would always be sufficient funds in this account every time the bill is due. If the bill is due on a certain date, and there isn't enough money in your account to cover the cost, the ramifications would be great. The banking institution would charge you an insufficient funds charge for not having enough money in your account when the transition was initiated by the company to which you owe money.

And also, because you ultimately didn't pay the bill on time, the company to which you owe the money may charge you a late fee. It's common for the banking institution to have an "insurance-type" policy to protect you from ever having to worry about an insufficient funds situation – it's called overdraft protection.

Sometimes, there is a monthly charge for overdraft protection. It may be well worth the monthly charge for peace of mind. Sometimes, overdraft protection is a free service if you maintain a certain balance in your bank account or if you have multiple bank accounts "linked together" in the same bank. You'll have to ask your banker for the required forms to have this service established for you.

Another option is to pay bills over the Internet. This is becoming increasingly popular as more and more people are comfortable with conducting financial transactions via their home computers. Again, the company or utility to which you owe money has to offer this option. They will have a set of instructions and procedures for you to set up an account, user id, and password. Once the initial set up has been completed and you receive their bill, all you'll have to do is follow the company's instructions and pay the bill online. Those who use this service say it's really easy. Sometimes they qualify for discounts because they pay using the Internet. Plus they save on the cost of stamps.

There are still some people who may not have a checking account or perhaps live or work near the bill payment location for a certain company and elect to pay the bill in person. As long as the bill payment location is not out of your way, this is an option you may find works best for you.

Whichever bill payment option you use – and you very well may utilize not only one, but a number of these options, depending on what the companies offer – get into the routine of paying your bills on a regular, routine basis. And vow to never pay any bills late, at least not because of being neglectful. By vowing to never pay bills late, you will potentially save hundreds or thousands of dollars over time, compared to those who pay their bills in a haphazard manner.

Eating Meals Together

Grace isn't a little prayer you chant before receiving a meal.
It's a way to live.

– *Jackie Windspear*

Unfortunately for society, eating meals at the same time and in the same place has swiftly become a thing of the past. As a newly married couple, it's important to create a tradition of having a sit down, family style meal where you can share in each other's days and reconnect.

Not only do family meals strengthen your relationship, but a number of studies that have been done throughout the years have shown that families who sit at the table and have meals together eat healthier, more nutritious meals.

Think about it; those who eat on the run typically wind up in a drive-thru window and eat their fattening, high-calorie "food" in one of two places: in the car, or in front of the television.

There is just something about having that special mealtime as a family unit that brings out the health conscious side to almost anyone. When eating on the run, or away from the rest of your family, you pay little attention to what's on your plate or how much of it you consume. Eating in front of other people, or while enjoying stimulating, bonding conversation, makes you more aware of what actually goes on your fork and into your mouth.

In addition, when considering the prepa-

ration of an actual meal, most people will include protein, starch, vegetables, and fruit instead of a burger with fries cooked in artery clogging saturated oils.

Here are some tricks to keep mealtime alive and enjoyable in your home:

* Mealtime can include any meal. With today's hectic schedules, most of us only think of dinner, regarding the family meal. But a family meal can be breakfast, lunch, or dinner.

* Plan meals for the week in advance. Mark your calendar and decide before the week begins which meals you will have together. Try to plan one at least every other day, but one meal every day would be ideal.

* Keep quick meal ingredients on hand. You don't have to slave over a hot stove for hours to have a family meal. A good, healthy meal can be prepared in an hour or 30 minutes or less.

* Plan your meals before you do your shopping. When you make your shopping list, plan what will be prepared for each family meal, and purchase what is needed all at once. It's much easier to pass by the drive thru if you know that you already have the ingredients at home for your meal.

* Turn off all electronics. This includes the television, personal digital assistants (PDA's), cell phones, pagers, and anything else that may be a distraction. Make this time a time for you and your partner, and not for anyone in the outside world. Put the focus on your partner, and/or your family during mealtime. Create a tradition of mealtime as your family grows.

* Make the crock pot your friend. It's so easy to prepare a stew, roast or chili in the crock pot and have it ready when you arrive home. Get up a little earlier, prepare your ingredients, and arrive home to a slow-cooked, home cooked meal. It's that easy!

* Enjoy your time together. Although this time is time to catch up, it's not the time to rehash last night's argument, or to bring up accusations or negative topics. Make mealtime enjoyable with light conversation and fun so that you'll both look forward to it. This is your time to be together - relax, unwind, share, connect, enjoy, light some candles. You can be married and still dine by candlelight!

Keep the conversations flowing while the candle is glowing and be genuinely interested in what's going on in each other's lives.

To keep mealtime alive in your home, remind your family of the benefits of sharing meals. The following are just a few:

- It's cheaper to cook at home than to eat out.
- You'll keep the lines of communication open.
- You can actually reduce your waistband by being conscious about what you eat.
- Your dining room table won't collect dust.
- You can take turns practicing the art of cooking in the kitchen.
- As your family grows, your children will learn table manners and how to sit at a table and not use mealtime as playtime.
- Your children will learn how to cook and how to relate to their future spouses by watching you. As they grow older, let your daughters and sons help in the kitchen, too.
- You'll eat healthier.
- Your family will be closer, having spent many hours together conversing and catching up on what is missed.

If I haven't already convinced you to make mealtime a priority in your home, consider the fact that family meals are where most of the bonding takes place, where most communication is exchanged, and where strong family ties are created. The family that eats together stays together.

Hiring Domestic Help

Nature abhors a vacuum. And so do I.

– Anne Gibbons

Are you planning to clean the house yourself, or does the thought of cleaning the kitchen and bathrooms make you cringe? Are you considering hiring domestic help on a periodic basis? There are many ways to go about doing this.

You could hire a maid service to clean your house monthly, quarterly or for only special occasions and supplement those good, thorough cleanings by cleaning the house on your own. Or on the other end of the spectrum, you could hire a maid service on a weekly basis.

Consider the cost of hiring a maid service. If you have the means to do so, then do so. But if this is going to be a strain on the household budget, get your mop and your duster and do it yourself! You should not consider this kind of service, or luxury, if you really can't afford it.

If you're a do-it-yourselfer, or you can't find any wiggle room in your budget, or you're simply excited about cleaning your own home, here are some tips to help you keep your home clean:

* Always put away what you get out. Clutter is oftentimes the underlying reason behind a dirty home.

* Don't leave dirty dishes in the sink. Wash your dishes right away so you don't create the dreaded pile that you put off washing, or argue over whose turn it is to do the dishes.

* Clean one room a day. By making time each day to clean one room in the house, you'll always be caught up on your cleaning and you won't feel overwhelmed facing an entire dirty house.

* Wash at least one load each day and put away the clothes after they come out of the dryer instead of creating piles of laundry to fold.

* Clean one closet each month.

* De-clutter your life by resisting the urge to purchase or save stuff you really don't need.

* Share the cleaning. If you're cleaning a room a day, make time to clean it together. This will prevent one partner from getting stuck with all of the cleaning.

Whether you decide to clean your home yourself or hire someone to clean it for you, do what's right for you, your budget, and your time allowance.

Mail

*Letter writing is the only device for combining
solitude with good company.*

– Lord Byron

This is an area that is often underestimated in its importance. It is seldom discussed, but mail management is a very important matter to be handled in the management of a household. Who takes in the mail?

It sounds simple, and maybe it is for you. Do you have a designated person in your home that always gets the mail? Does the first one home for the day take the mail in? Is someone usually home at the time the mail is delivered every day; thus, you naturally retrieve the mail on a daily basis?

What if you don't have a routine setup? You may go several days without the mail being collected. In many cases, that may not really be that big of a deal. But, in the case of time-sensitive mail, that could prove to be a significant issue.

Talk about establishing a mail collection routine – whatever works for you. It doesn't have to be firmly delegated, but whatever you decide, it must be consistent.

Now that you know who will collect the mail, where is the mail placed, and how is it sorted? Again, this seems simple, but if it is not mutually discussed and agreed upon, the potential for adverse situations regarding your mail could increase drastically.

For instance, let's say Susan and Bill decides that the first one home for the day gets the mail. On Monday Susan arrives home first, gets the mail and places it on the night stand in the bedroom. On Tuesday, Bill arrives home first, gets the mail and places it on the stereo in the living room. On Wednesday, Bill arrives home first again, gets the mail and as soon as he opens the door, the phone starts ringing so he steps in the office to get the phone and places the mail he's holding on the desk. On Thursday, Susan gets home first and brings the mail in. She's so thirsty that she goes straight to the refrigerator for some bottled water and places the mail down on the kitchen countertop. On Friday, Susan gets home first, gets the mail and places it on her dresser as she changes into some relaxing clothes for the evening.

Okay, you get the point! The good news is that both Susan and Bill are consistent about the first one home retrieving the mail. Yippee! However, they don't have any kind of routine for where the mail goes once it's in the house. This will definitely lead to problems.

What if the car insurance bill was in Tuesdays' mail? It's on the stereo in the living room. If Bill forgets where he placed the mail on Tuesday and Susan doesn't happen to see it on the stereo, the car insurance is in jeopardy of not being paid on time. I don't know about you, but my luck is such that the day after the car insurance runs out, I'll be stopped at a random checkpoint with an expired car insurance card to show the police officer!

Many insurance companies will honor the same rates as long as you don't let the insurance policy lapse. If you let the insurance policy expire and then try to renew it, either your rates may increase or you may have to pay a penalty in order to reinstate it, or both. The insurance company may even tell you that they simply will not renew your policy, which means that you'll now have to shop around for another insurance company.

So, this simple act of not having an established place for the mail once collected and brought in the house could become very costly. Not to mention the cost of the ticket you got from the police officer at the checkpoint for not being insured, or worse if your automobile is impounded. We don't even want to go there, but do you see the potential for costly consequences from not properly executing such a simple chore?

Therefore, in addition to establishing a routine for the retrieval of the mail, you also need to establish a place where the mail will be placed once it's in your home.

You might elect to put it in a "mail" basket on the desk in your office or bedroom. Or you may choose to place it on the kitchen counter next to the toaster.

It doesn't matter where you decide to put the mail. What matters is that there is one place, and only one place, where all mail gets placed by either or both of you, every day.

Sorting the Mail

You may want to consider pre-sorting the mail. Pre-sorting may help make things easier in the long run.

What's pre-sorting? Let's say you develop five or six piles of mail. One pile could be for household or joint bills. The second pile could be for important mail to be read and/or saved, but are not bills. For instance, insurance documents, financial statements, and announcements from work may fall into this category. The third and fourth piles may be the "his and hers" piles for personal mail. The fifth pile may be for mail that may be informal; mail that you want to read but is not time sensitive. Magazines and publications would fit into this category. The remaining mail may not be so important to you and you may be able to go through it quickly to decide whether or not you want to keep it at all. If it's so-called junk mail, throw it away as you're sorting. Nothing can make your mail pile grow out of control faster than a pile of junk mail. It's best to handle it once and just get rid of it, rather than putting it in a pile just to throw it away later.

It doesn't take long to pre-sort the mail, especially if it's done on a daily basis before it piles up and becomes a bigger task to take on. The benefit of pre-sorting is that if Susan wants to only see her personal mail, she can read the stack already piled up for her without having to peruse through the entire stack, including Bill's personal mail, bills she knows she's not going to pay at this time, magazines and periodicals, letters, and statements from financial and insurance institutions, etc. And, when Bill is ready to pay the bills, he only has the stack of bills that were previously pre-sorted to deal with.

Other Necessary Chores

You sometimes see a woman who would have made a Joan of Arc in another century and climate, threshing herself to pieces over all the mean worry of housekeeping.

– *Rudyard Kipling*

$\mathcal{W}$e've already covered most of the household topics, but there are still a few chores that will need to be delegated, otherwise, how will they get done? So let's cover the rest of the necessary tasks that make a house run smoothly and feel like a home.

- Shopping – Who will do the shopping in your home? This doesn't just include grocery shopping. Things like household goods, cleaning supplies, pet food and supplies, and other general things will need to be purchased on a regular basis. It helps if you keep a list in plain sight, such as on your refrigerator, so that each of you can write down the things that you're low on or out of in your home. Work at creating your shopping list before you go to the store, and stick to what's on your list. Impulsive purchases are usually the things that will break your budget. Decide what you need and how much you can afford to spend before leaving your home.

- Washing Dishes – Typically, whoever does the cooking doesn't have to do the dishes. If you have a designated chef in your home, then the other person is usually the one to clean up. If you do the dishes immediately following your family mealtime, then make a plan to clean up together. The job gets done much faster and is much more enjoyable if you have help. Many hands make light work! (Sidebar – I can't believe I used that phrase! I remember as a child growing up, my father would call my sister and me downstairs to help him and my mother prepare dinner. On this particular day, I must have had something that I thought was important to do and preparing dinner was not at all desirable. I obviously came downstairs with a scowl on my face that my father immediately picked up on. He said for the millionth time, "Many hands make light work." I replied in a very low tone, under my breath, purposely inaudible (my parents didn't raise a fool!), "Too many cooks spoil the broth!")

But, I digress…

* Cleaning bathrooms – We've already covered how to maintain a clean home, but bathrooms are often the cause for heated discussions. Plan to clean the bathroom at least once a week or whatever frequency suits you best. Remember, the more often you clean, the less dirty it gets.

* Dusting – Again, by dusting a room each day, you'll be ahead of the dust and it won't become a huge chore. Break your housework into small chunks and share the load. Anyone can climb a mountain (or reach any goal) – one step at a time.

* Emptying the garbage – This chore is typically the man's, but unless your garbage can is a long distance from your door, or your garbage is exceptionally heavy, this chore can be shared by the two of you. If it's his turn to cook, she can take out the trash after she's washed the dishes, and vice versa.

* Making the bed – A good rule of thumb in bed making is the last one out gets to make the bed. If she leaves for work at 6am and he sleeps until 8am, then he should make the bed. Make the bed as soon as you get out of it and it won't be one of those dreaded chores that "have to be done." It will become automatic or natural, always being accomplished yet never requiring any thought.

* Pets and related chores – Another good rule of thumb is "you own it, you feed it." Usually, especially in the case of newlyweds, a pet belongs to one partner or the other. Rarely do partners share equally in the love, caring and nurturing of a pet (That is unless both of you are animal lovers or you get your pet after you've been together). She may have a cat, while he has a dog. But it's never a good situation to assume he fed the cat or she fed the dog. Have a plan for pet care and stick to it. Pets depend on us to see to their needs. So take responsibility for the care of your pets as you would your child.

- Maintenance and Outdoor – Traditionally, the outdoor chores are done by the "man of the house." But, oftentimes gender has little to do with who in the family enjoys taking care of outdoor chores and who has the time to do it. She may be the one with the green thumb and enjoys doing some or most of the outdoor chores. If you live in an apartment or condo, usually the outdoor chores are performed by a maintenance crew and neither of you have to worry about doing anything. If you live in a home or a townhouse that has a yard, you may want to have a discussion and decide if either of you will be responsible for the upkeep or if you can afford to hire a service to do it for you. Again, figure out what works best for you and your budget.

- Washing Clothes and Ironing – Washing and ironing clothes can be a tedious job, but it has to be done. If you can afford to use a laundry service, then the only thing to decide is who will drop off and pick up the clothes. If you can't afford one, or you live in a remote area where there are none within close vicinity, or you simply have no desire to use a laundry service, then you must decide who will be responsible for making sure the laundry is done.

Male Chores and Female Expectations
Female Chores and Male Expectations

This is a honeydew day. That is when you get a day off and the wife says,
"Honey, do this," and "Honey, do that" around the house.

– Jim Lemon

This is a touchy subject and you must be very careful when discussing who will do which chores within your household. It's easy to assume that the wife will take care of all the cooking and cleaning while the husband does the yard work and maintains the car. That's how it was in decades passed. However, times have changed and so have gender roles within the household.

Many young couples who are just starting out live in apartments or condos where there are no outside chores to be done. Some wives are the breadwinners of the home. It's important to fully understand and come to an agreement of what is expected of each partner before you get married and move in together. Do not allow gender or societal expectations to dictate who will do what. The last thing you want to do is offend your partner by assuming he or she will take care of a chore just because of their gender.

Follow the previous guidelines for assigning responsibility to each chore and take into consideration things like time, experience, and desire to complete a chore to help you decide who will be the responsible party.

Questions to Ask Before Taking the Leap

1. Do you have an idea of what chores will need to be done for your household?

2. How will you decide who does what?

3. Do you have a clear picture of what you really can afford if you choose to hire help?

4. Do you and your fiancé/spouse share similar views on your respective roles regarding housework?

5. Do you think it will be difficult to establish a compromise regarding your housework duties and chores?

6. Will one of you simply adapt the views of the other partner and accept them?

7. Are there certain household chores that you simply refuse to do under any circumstance?

8. Does your fiancé/spouse perform certain chores absolutely wrong, in your opinion?

9. Do you honestly hold up to your end of the bargain regarding chores and maintaining your household according to what both of you agreed?

10. Are you happy or satisfied with how your household is maintained?

Notes, thoughts, ideas, questions and issues I want to discuss with my love...

Chapter Ten

Goals

If you don't know where you are going,
you will probably end up somewhere else.

– Lawrence J. Peter

*W*ithout goals, there is no clear path to where you and your partner are headed in life. It's like going on a long trip without a map. How do you know which way to turn when you pull out of your driveway?

Goals create happiness in life. If you think back to times when you were sad, depressed or bored, you'll most likely realize that it was during those times that you weren't working towards something to better yourself; you weren't doing anything in relation to realizing a dream.

Consider this: without a goal, even the least significant one, what do you have to look forward to? What are you working toward if not for something? What reason do you have to wake up day after day and to go to a job that you dislike without having something that you're working toward?

A goal can be something small like getting the house clean, or something big like saving for a down payment on a new home. No matter the size of the goal, you always want to be able to look into the future and see something that you're working towards achieving; a reason to get up every day and get something done.

Not only is it important to have a path set for your goals, but you and your partner must also be headed down the same path. The following are some tips to ensure your goals will be compatible with your partners'.

* Make a list of the goals you have not reached as individuals.
* Make a list of the goals you would like to reach as a couple.
* Write the goals in order of their importance to you.
* Compare your individual goals to your expected goals as a couple.
* Discuss any differences in your goals.
* Compromise on major goal differences.
* Determine that you will work together towards your goals. Don't compete with each other.

By having your goals decided upon at the onset of your marriage, you'll have a clear path to follow on your daily lives together. Remember to check off your goals as you achieve them and continue to add new goals to your list. Keep your goals in mind whenever making life changing or financial decisions and always discuss with your partner any new goals along the way.

Questions to Ask Before Taking the Leap

1. Have you made a list of your individual goals?
2. Have you made a list of goals you would like to share as a couple?
3. Are you willing to compromise on different ideas of what your goals should be?
4. Have you communicated your goals clearly to your fiancé?
5. Historically, are you good at working towards goals that you've set for yourself?
6. How do you and your fiancé/spouse accept support from each other?
7. Are you or would you be supportive if your fiancé/spouse requested your help?
8. Do you inspire and motivate each other regarding your common goals?
9. Do you feel a responsibility to yourself and your fiancé/spouse to follow through on your commitments regarding your common goals?
10. If your spouse did not follow through on a commitment towards one of your common goals.
    a) What would you do?
    b) How would you support them?
11. Do you work well together?

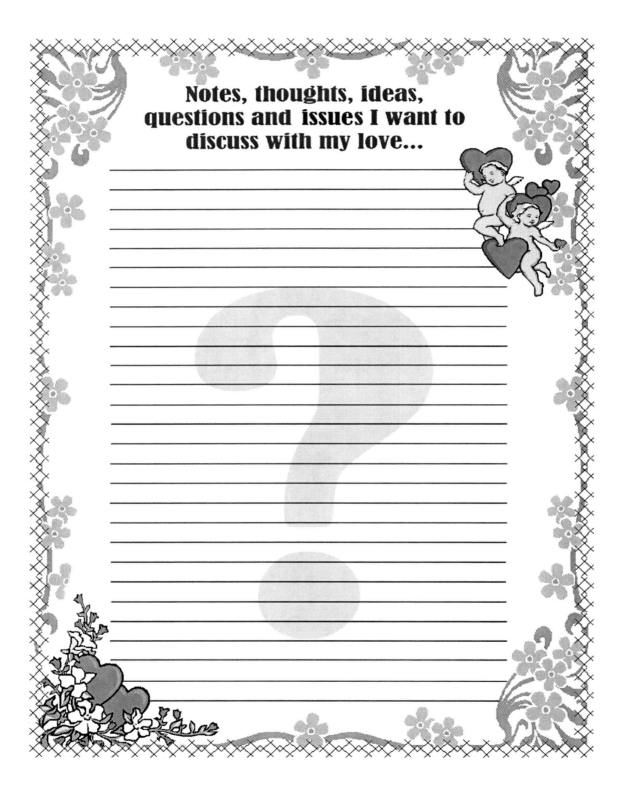

Notes, thoughts, ideas, questions and issues I want to discuss with my love...

Chapter Eleven

Career

Every day I get up and look through the Forbes
list of the richest people in America.
If I'm not there, I go to work.

– Robert Orben

*L*ong gone are the days when one income fully supported the majority of the households in America. Now it's most likely that a family will be a two income family with both partners working full-time jobs rather than for one spouse to work inside the home while the other works outside the home.

At parties and social gatherings, the first question asked of attendees is, "What do you do?" It's just assumed that you have a career or a job and that you don't stay at home. But what about the millions of moms who take on the role of housewife and full-time mom? Or, what about the dads who choose to stay home while the mom earns a living?

Choosing a career over your family, or vice versa, is a hard decision to make. Those who stay at home versus entering or remaining in the workforce oftentimes feel powerless. They may feel as though their contributions to the family are far inferior to that of their spouse. Though on paper this might be the case, in actuality, the partner at home is usually the one with the 24/7 job maintaining the family and household while the working partner puts in their time at the job and goes home to relax. It's for these reasons that post-nuptials have recently gained popularity.

Post-nuptials put an end to any future arguments about who contributes what to the family, and puts the stay at home partner at ease about their financial future in case of a possible break up. If you or your spouse decides to forego a career, it will depend on your relationship, communication, and trust for each other to decide whether or not a post-nuptial is even necessary. (A post-nuptial agreement is a legal contract between married spouses. It contains many of the same elements that a pre-nuptial contains, except that it is agreed upon and signed after you're already married.) Following is a list of questions to ask yourself before you make the decision to stay home versus to pursue a career:

* Can you handle being home every day?
* Could you tolerate a minimum amount of adult conversation?

- Can you handle full-time parental duties?
- Do you enjoy taking care of the home?

If you answered "yes" to all of the above questions, then staying home may fit in with your lifestyle. But if "no" was the predominate answer, you may at least consider working part-time or volunteering a few hours a week if staying at home is a necessity for your family.

Balancing Home and Career

The difference between a job and a career is the difference between forty and sixty hours a week.

– Robert Frost

Balancing your career with your home life is not always an easy task to achieve. As newlyweds, this is something that won't come naturally and will take some work from both of you.

Before you got married, working a sixty-hour work week probably seemed like nothing and you didn't have to consider anyone else's schedule or plans. But now that you're married, you and/or your partner may have a different idea of what your weekly work hours should be.

There has to be a balance that works for both of you as a couple. On one hand, working extra hours may be great for saving money to purchase your first home. On the other hand, you're newlyweds trying to establish a life together. Now is not the best time to always be at work and never be at home.

You must strive to find the balance that works for you and your partner. What you think is a good amount of time to spend at work, (away from home), may not be what your partner thinks. Yes, your career is important, and you may want to or have to devote extra time to your career. But your family is also very important.

Your family needs your devotion, too. Either way you look at it you don't want to concentrate on one to the point of neglecting the other. Balance is crucial!

I have a friend who recently got married. Before the wedding, he would work as much overtime as he could, saving and investing much of his income for the future. Now that he's married, he and his wife jointly decided that the overtime, double time, back-to-back shifts and weekend work were not as important as spending time together. They decided that some overtime is great, but they agreed that he would not work weekend hours anymore.

I have another friend whose wife quit her job shortly after they were married. She decided she wanted to stay home and be a full-time housewife. However, she didn't share this with her husband until after she'd already quit her job! She simply thought that was the way it was supposed to be. Her mother never worked and this was quite natural to her. He went ballistic! It never even crossed his mind that he'd be the sole provider in his new household. How could she do this without talking to him about it first?

Many people will agree that the first years of a marriage are the most difficult. It's in the first year or years of marriage that so many things are changing for each of you. These big changes may include housing, becoming more serious about your career, debt from the wedding and reception, and getting used to sharing daily life with your partner. Some people literally go from being single apartment renters to married, home owners, and then parents in a year – or less. I call all of these things happening seemingly at once, "turbo life." It can be overwhelming to have your entire life and everything that you once knew, change so quickly.

Communicate with your partner and be honest about your feelings about the changes that will undoubtedly take place. Your new wife or husband is probably feeling similarly, and by discussing, addressing and resolving the situation(s) together; your bond will grow even stronger.

Questions to Ask Before Taking the Leap

1. Have you openly discussed whether both of you will maintain careers?

2. Do you consider it necessary or desirable for one of you stay home and do the housework and/or raise your children?

3. Will you need two incomes to support your family?

4. Have you discussed a post-nuptial agreement in case one of you decides to stay home?

5. Which would you rank as higher in importance?

   a)   a satisfying career?

   b)   earning enough to satisfy your family's financial goals?

6. Would you ever consider changing careers?

7. Would you support your fiancé/spouse if they wanted to change careers?

8. How would you feel if your spouse would not receive a salary or an income, or had to take a reduction in pay for a period of time in order for them to change their career?

9. Would you consider continuing your education to obtain a new degree or specialized training in order to qualify for advancement in your current career or to change careers?

10. If your spouse informed you they wanted to leave their job or career in order to start their own business, would you be supportive?

11. Does your career define you?

Notes, thoughts, ideas, questions and issues I want to discuss with my love...

Chapter Twelve

Relationship Matters

*One of the major barriers in communication is the
unspoken expectations that a couple has of one another.
Honestly appraise your expectations of yourself, your spouse,
and your marriage. Are they realistic or unrealistic?*

– Reginald Wickham

Communication

Communication is one of the most significant components in a relationship. Communication consists of speaking clearly and consistently listening. There is a famous saying that goes, "You have two ears and one mouth for a very good reason." That reason is, if you listen twice as much as you speak, you probably will be a better communicator. It's imperative that you become a good listener in order to be a good communicator.

Another extremely important component of communication is to be sure to ask for what you want. And the converse is just as important, if not more so; it's imperative to understand that you are not a mind reader. It's a dangerous practice to believe that you can read what's on your partner's mind or interpret his or her body language 100% of the time.

Similarly, your partner will not be able to read what's on your mind. It's impossible – we are not mind readers. Even if we think we know each other very well, we're not capable of reading what's on one another's mind.

The best way to know what's on your partner's mind is to ask your partner! Similarly, if your partner wants to know what's on your mind, your partner needs to ask you.

If you attempt to "read" your partner's mind, you may be correct – this time. In other words, you may have guessed correctly in this particular case. The danger is, this leads to a false sense of your mind reading ability. If you continue the practice of attempting to read your partner's mind, inevitably, you'll miss the mark, perhaps more times than not.

Another word for mind reading is "assuming." Now, if you're in the practice of confirming with your partner what you've just assumed, your partner will then have the opportunity to confirm your hypothesis. If you assumed incorrectly, your partner has the opportunity to correct you. You've given your partner the opportunity to make sure you're on the right track by asking them for feedback regarding your assumption.

If you must assume, or in other words if you insist on being a mind reader and you check in with your partner, you are receiving acknowledgment. Therefore, you've made an assumption and you've confirmed that your assumption is correct before acting on it.

The problem, however, comes to play when you don't check in with your partner. Problems with your assumptions occur when you make an assumption and hold it to be true without confirming with your partner whether it is actually true or not. This will undoubtedly lead to problems.

Even as well as you think you know each other, the best way to find out what's on your partner's mind is to simply ask. Not only is this the best way, it's the only way to be sure.

Developing good communications skills is an ongoing practice that will get better and better over time. As young children, most of us are naturally good communicators. Or at least kids are good at letting us know exactly what's on their mind and how they are feeling. But even those of us who start out as good communicators become socialized and actually learn or are carefully taught how to be bad communicators.

For instance, six year old Jeffrey may see a man with a huge hole in his jeans while shopping at the mall with his mother and siblings. What's Jeffrey likely to do? (We've all seen some variation of this). Jeffrey will tug on his mother, getting her attention and point at the man saying, "Look ma! That man has a hole in his pants!" Of course Jeffrey will shout out his amazing discovery and his mother will be mortified! She'll scold Jeffrey by telling him, "Be quiet! It's not polite to point and talk about people."

The mother acted appropriately because she's right! It's not polite to point at people and talk about them. But Jeffrey and his brothers and sisters are also learning another lesson; Jeffrey is learning to repress his ideas and feelings.

Children learn at an early age that it's not appropriate to speak honestly and they learn that when they tell the honest to goodness truth it can hurt someone's feelings; thus, the remedy, to a child, is to learn not to say anything at all.

Imagine this…

It's almost time to sit down to eat dinner and the phone rings. As eleven year old Brenda reaches to answer the phone her dad says, "Just find out who it is, but if it's for me, tell them I haven't come home from work yet." Brenda complies, hangs up, and the family sits down together for dinner. What happened here?

Well, the good news is that the family has made it their priority to sit down together to enjoy a meal. But the bad news is that Brenda, and any other siblings within earshot, just learned that it's okay to lie; it's okay to misrepresent the truth for the sake of convenience.

Lessons like these are part of a child's socialization. They learn many lessons every day and every year from parents, teachers, other figures of authority, friends, etc. Now, of course every lesson they learn is not a bad lesson. But some lessons that we teach our children, if you dissect them, could be harmful to a child developing communication skills.

Fast forward to when Jeffrey, Brenda, and a host of other children reach the stage when they're dating, and eventually marrying. How will they communicate with their partners? If they sometimes choose to lie or not say anything at all, concealing their true feelings, could you blame them? They've been carefully taught that if they say how they truly feel, they may be hurting the other person, or in this case, the one they love. Or, if it's somehow convenient for them to misrepresent the truth, well they've been taught that it's perfectly okay.

Attending interpersonal communication classes is a great way to learn how we currently communicate. You can learn to recognize your communication patterns, many of which you probably do without thinking, knowing or understanding why you do it.

Interpersonal communication classes also teach you how to practice better communication skills. You'll learn tools that can mold you from a bad or ineffective communicator into a good or effective communicator.

When both parties in the soon-to-be-married couple take interpersonal communication classes together, you'll both understand yourselves and each other so much better. You'll be able to speak the same language. But if only one of you take the time and effort to attend interpersonal communication classes, you'll likely be communicating on a much higher, or a different level.

Good communication skills are learned. Some of us pick up the skills within our own families and others learn from watching those who have mastered the art.

However, there is a significant portion of the population who didn't pay attention to our role models, or who had role models who were less competent in their communication skills. Some of us go about "communicating" without a clue.

Communication classes or training teach things such as:

* Sharing thoughts and feelings
* Listening
* Responding appropriately
* Considering the needs of others
* Compromise

Do you think you're a good communicator? Ask yourself these questions:

* Am I physically and mentally present when others are talking?
    * Do I convey my true feelings, while considering the feelings of others?
    * Do I think before I respond?
    * After angrily writing a harsh email that may cause an emotional, defensive response; do I sit down and cool off for a while - then reread it and edit it appropriately before clicking send?
    * When I receive emails and phone calls, do I respond in a timely manner, or do I postpone my response at the inconvenience of others?
    * Do I encourage my partner to communicate his or her feelings to me?
    * Am I responsive to my partner's feelings?
    * Am I open to negative communication and do I respond appropriately and not defensively?
    * Am I open to positive communication and do I respond appropriately?

Think about it…most problems that occur in a relationship or marriage can be circumvented if good communication skills are utilized, each party knows how to express themselves effectively, and they do so in an open, fair, and supportive environment. If you didn't answer "yes" to all of the previous questions, even if you answered "yes" to most of them, there is still room for improvement. Learn how to communicate with your partner early in your marriage. Communication will keep your marriage strong in good times and bad.

Honesty

If you tell the truth you don't have to remember anything.

– Mark Twain

Honesty is a huge component in a relationship. It's also a huge component in communication. If you and your partner are not honest with each other, then communication is futile.

When you ask your partner something, of course you would expect a truthful response. If your partner asks you a question and you *choose* to provide a response that is not true, your partner will be misled. If he or she senses that

you were dishonest, this can lead to feelings that you're not trustworthy. Your partner has lost the confidence that you are able or willing to tell the truth; to be honest. This is a horrible, horrible foundation on which to build a strong relationship.

Similarly, when you ask your partner a question, you're expecting an honest answer in return. If your partner chooses to answer you dishonestly, this can do nothing but lead to problems.

One of the ramifications of being labeled as one who doesn't tell the truth is your partner can't always decipher when you're being truthful from when you're not being truthful. And since you've already proven that you are capable of or sometimes choose to be untruthful, every response you give will be subject to suspicion. You've ruined your trust and integrity. You'll find yourself being questioned more and more.

You'll find yourself always having to verify, confirm or prove that what you said is true. This gets old for both partners. The partner who lost the feeling of trust for their spouse always feels like a spy – trying to catch their mate in a lie. And the other partner always feels as though they're constantly being interrogated. Is this how you want to live?

Effective communication in a relationship requires honesty from both partners. If your partner feels that you're not honest in your communication, you won't receive the support, love and respect that you desire in your relationship.

Love

The hunger for love is much more
difficult to remove than the hunger for bread.

– Mother Teresa

Give love to your partner in every way and as often as you can. Learn ways that your fiancé wants and needs to receive love – then fulfill them.

If you don't already know yourself, get to know yourself. Then share with your partner ways in which you want and need to be loved. When you receive love from your partner, learn if you must, to receive it lovingly. Acknowledge the fact that he or she thought of you so much that they demonstrated their love for you.

If your partner gives you love in ways that suits him or her but not you, thank them for loving you in that special way. Share, perhaps at another time, ways in which you also would like to or need to receive love. Then, love your partner some more.

Here's an example. Marcy is a natural caregiver. She's the oldest in a family of five children and happens to enjoy taking care of those she loves. David is a loving guy as well. He's very independent having grown up as an only child.

Just married, David is getting ready for work. He can't understand why Marcy lays out his clothes for him. He's not a child. He's been dressing himself since he was eight years old. He never wears what Marcy lays out for him, expressing his independence.

Marcy, on the other hand, can't understand why David is being such a knucklehead! She went through the trouble every morning for a week to lay out his clothes for him before she prepares for work herself and he purposely wears something else! How cruel! How thoughtless!

When they get home, touchy, feely David wants to cuddle up to Marcy and hold hands as they discuss what happened during the day. Marcy, gently at first, tries to brush his hands off of her. She just got home and has things to get done. Marcy is thinking, "Why is he being such a pain. All he wants is sex! Well not right now!" And David is thinking, "Gees, I'm just trying to be affectionate. Why is Marcy so cold?"

Marcy and David simply have different ways in which they express love and need love in return. If they understand how they express love and need love for themselves and each other they'll learn to appreciate how their partner expresses love and how to love their partner.

Love for one another can be expressed in limitless ways. Here are just a few suggestions:

- Love can be expressed in simple, subtle ways, like holding hands or looking into each other's eyes.

- A loving gesture can be to send your fiancé a card expressing your love, and not because of a birthday or a holiday, but just because.

- Love can also be expressed by taking your partner out to his or her favorite restaurant to celebrate a holiday or a significant event or milestone. Or it can be expressed by learning to cook a favorite meal.

- Love can be expressed by repairing the lampshade you've been hearing about for several weeks.

- Love can be expressed by washing your partner's car, just because you were thinking of them.

- Love can be expressed by saving up enough of your overtime pay for a night on the town without having to borrow from your monthly budget.

- Love can be expressed by letting your partner invite his or her favorite friends over while you give them the space they need.

- Love can be contributing to a travel fund all year only to present your partner with the trip he or she always wanted to take.

- Love can be expressed by praying together.

- Love can be expressed by showing interest or appreciation in something that your mate is deeply involved in.

- Love can be expressed by listening to your partner.

Find creative ways to love your partner. When you find one, do it. Then find some more.

Forgiveness

Once a woman has forgiven her man,
she must not reheat his sins for breakfast.

– Marlene Dietrich

Forgiving your partner is one of the hardest things you'll ever do. To truly forgive someone for something, you must also learn not to keep bringing it up. Has your partner done anything up until this point that you forgave him or her for but you still are haunted with painful memories each time the subject is brought up? Where did the pain come from? Was it something done against you? Were there words spoken out of spite? Or was it an act that severed the trust in your relationship?

In order to move past the hurt and the feelings of betrayal, you must let go of the actions and realize that your significant other is not perfect and that mistakes will be made along the way. The following are the steps to forgiveness. If you're already carrying around pain in your relationship, that pain can slowly eat away the bonds of trust in your marriage until there is nothing left. Start with forgiving your partner for any prior actions and build a new relationship from this point forward. Work through these steps each time there is a reason to forgive or be forgiven and your foundation will be solid and your marriage will be strong.

Steps for the forgiver:

* Before a heated argument erupts, take some time for yourself and think about what it was in your partner's actions that hurt you. Was the hurt from words? Was it from actions? What did your partner do that would constitute the need for forgiveness?

* Once you've taken time for yourself to think about the event, decide whether or not the event is something that you can forgive. Was it a huge indiscretion like infidelity, or something minor like leaving the top off the toothpaste? What was the magnitude of the event and is it something that in your heart you could ever truly forgive?

- If you have doubts that you can truly forgive, seek counseling for the matter. Ask someone outside your relationship, such as clergy or a counselor, to discuss the event with you to decide if it's something that is really a major event or actually something minor that you've magnified in your mind (Keep in mind that during this step it's never a good idea to involve family or friends in your disagreements. If you are willing to forgive your partner, your family and friends most likely will not. They love you and want only happiness for you and it could put a strain on the relationship between your partner and your other loved ones. However, if the event was something unforgivable, such as any form of abuse whether verbal, emotional or physical, your family and friends do need to know what's going on in your relationship. In those times, they're the ones you should turn to for support).

- After you've decided that the event was something forgivable, it's time to sit down and communicate with your partner. Express your true feelings of how the event affected you. Allow your partner to see the hurt that's been caused so that there is no reoccurrence, but assure him or her that the event will never be brought up again if the action that caused the hurt goes away and never returns.

- Show your love and respect for your partner. After communicating your feelings and "burying the hatchet," do something as a couple that will allow you both the time to bond and heal. If you enjoy sports, do a sporting activity together. If you like to go to the movies, see something inspirational. Or you can just take a walk on the beach or around the park, hold hands, and discuss your plans for the future. Put the hurt aside and remember what you love about your partner.

- Don't dwell on the past. Release it. Get over it. And move together into the future. If you continue to think about the hurt that was caused, you'll only open up fresh wounds. Let it go!

- Live in the present and look towards the future. Don't rehash the past. Whenever you have conversations from this point forward, make them about the future and don't bring up anything you might regret saying later. If you find yourself in an argument, don't use things that were forgiven as ammunition against your partner. Look forward, not behind.

* Be intimate! The best way to show your love for your partner, and build your trust, is to be as intimate as possible. Touch each other deeply and share a bonding experience together.

* Keep the lines of communication open. If your partner does anything that causes you to doubt his or her actions, say so! Let your partner know that what's being said or done is not creating a bond of trust in your relationship. Many times, things are said or done without thoughts as to how it affects the partner. Bring these hurtful things to light and move on from there.

Steps for the forgiven:

* The first step is to STOP whatever it is you're doing or have done that is causing hurt. STOP the action and take some time to think about what it is you've done.

* If necessary, seek counseling. Discover why it is you did what you did. Was it subconscious? Were you purposely trying to hurt your partner? What drove you to do what you did? You must know what caused the action before you can ask forgiveness. Otherwise, you could possibly do it again. If you can't figure out what caused it, get help.

* Is the action something that can be forgiven? Was it something minor or did you really mess up? What was the magnitude of the action? Does your partner know what you did? Is the action something that you've explored and affirmed never to do again? If you've alleviated the problem, you know you won't repeat the action, and your partner doesn't know about it, is it something he or she needs to know? You must be careful here because if the action was something that your partner didn't know about, will telling your partner only relieve your conscious, but hurt the one you love? It's important to clarify that relieving your conscious doesn't make your relationship stronger. If you're seeking to relieve your conscious, discuss your action with a member of the clergy or a

therapist and explore whether or not you should tell your part-ner about the action. If the action was unforgivable and came in the form of abuse, seek counseling immediately!! Deciding to end abusive behavior on your own will not work no matter how hard you try! If you've been abusive, separate from your partner and get help before you attempt to amend any wrongdoing.

* If your action is something you've decided to discuss with your partner, communicate honestly and openly and allow your partner to know the "why" behind your actions. If he or she knows the "why," and that you've discovered and taken care of the "why," it should also be known that you're working towards never repeat-ing the action again. Without knowing the "why," your partner will always have doubts as to whether or not you're going to repeat the action sometime in the future.

* You must also consider the following: What if you decided not to tell your partner what you did. Then, sometime in the future your partner finds out. The problem has now become significantly com-pounded. Your partner not only has to deal with whatever it is you did, but they also have to deal with the fact that you chose to cover it up or hide it from them; effectively lying to them about it.

* Once you've been forgiven, move forward in your relationship with the same steps as the forgiver. Work to develop a stronger, closer, and more intimate relationship than you had before this point. Look toward the future and not the past and be patient if it takes some time for your partner to heal.

Patience

Patience is the ability to tolerate waiting, delay, or aggravation without becoming annoyed, frustrated, upset, and to continue calmly when faced with difficulties.

– Definition from Wikipedia

This is one of the keys to a great relationship. If you were to ask 100 couples who have a great, long-lasting relationship what "secrets" they have or advice they can give attesting to their longevity, without doubt, patience will be one of the main ingredients that they collectively agree upon.

In our current society with instant gratification being the norm for everything, patience is becoming a lost art. From fast food to super fast Internet connections, from aggressive job deadlines to speed dating…we, as a society, are accustomed to having everything at our finger tips, NOW!

When we experience a situation where things are not as fast as we think they should be, we get very anxious. No? Don't believe me? How do you feel when you're waiting in traffic? How do you feel when you click on a link on the Internet and the page takes a "long time" to appear? How do you feel when you're waiting in line at the grocery store or the person in front of you requires a price check? How do you feel when your significant other had said he or she was going to wash the dishes after dinner and yet the dishes are still there two days later?

Learn to be patient. In the Bible there is a verse that says something to the effect of "patience is a virtue," and it truly is. If you learn patience, you're relationship will be oh so much better because of it!

Acceptance

Acceptance, usually refers to the experience of a situation without an intention to change that situation, or loving someone without an intention to change them.

– Definition from Wikipedia

Acceptance is another one of those ever important keys to a good relationship. If you don't accept your loved one for who they are, you'll forever try to change them, mold them, and make them into the person you want them to be.

I hear so often that "Once we're married, he'll settle down." Yeah right! If your partner hasn't fully committed to you before now, forget it! Vows have no magical powers and they won't turn your hyperactive puppy into a well-trained docile dog. Leopards don't change their spots. So you have to get this straight before you say your "I do's." Know that whomever you choose to be with for the rest of your life is who you will get. Not some better, neater, tamer, more respectful version of the person you love.

Don't get me wrong, people do change, grow and mature and living together day in and day out will make your bond stronger. But all those little habits that seem "cute" now could become annoying when dealing with them day, after day, after day. So you must be willing to accept your partner for who he or she is now, not what you alone foresee in their future. Without acceptance and realization, you'll be doomed to wake up five years down the road and realize that nothing has changed and you're tired of it.

Accept your loved one for whom they really are, and not what you think they can become. If you don't accept them, disappointment can only follow.

Appreciation

In the opinion of the world, marriage ends all, as it does in a comedy.
The truth is precisely the opposite: it begins all.

– Anne Sophie Swetchine

Why do we sometimes treat the one we love worse than anyone else? We may be kind to our friends, even though they did something to get on our nerves. We may be gentle to our parents and in-laws, even though they did or said something that got under our skin - again! We're kind to our co-workers and bosses, even though we can't wait until Friday so we don't have to see them for a couple of days.

We all have relationships where we have been taught and trained to be kind, no matter what. Then we come home to the person we love and chose to spend the rest of our lives with, and we treat them horribly - taking out all of our anger and frustration built up during the day. Huh?

How is that fair? And why do we do that? Maybe it's because we feel powerless in our other relationships. Maybe it's because we can be our honest selves in front of our spouse and we don't have to put on an act. If we feel horrible, we act horrible.

I say it really doesn't matter why we do it. It's important to recognize when we do it and then do whatever it takes to stop doing it! If you're capable of stopping it on your own, then stop! If you feel you need some help learning how to channel your anger constructively - get help.

You should strive to treat your spouse with love and respect - always! And, your spouse should make it his or her mission to treat you with love and respect - always. Period!

Compromise

A compromise is an art of keeping others happy for our own happiness.

– Rosie Cash

Don't compromise yourself. You're all you've got.

– Janis Joplin

*W*hat is compromise?

If you need to compromise that means there is something that you're discussing with each other on which you don't agree. One of you feels one way about the issue and the other one feels another way about it - and both ways, apparently, can not co-exist. A compromise is a negotiated agreement or "settlement" wherein both of you agree to "give up" something that you want while "keeping" other things that you want in order to sort of meet somewhere in the middle. A compromise is a cordial, respectful, give and take process with a goal of both parties being satisfied or, at least, both parties being able to live with the outcome.

Let's say both of you agree that you need to purchase a new car. One of you has your mind set on a pricey, luxury, roomy SUV with all of the latest safety features to put you at ease since you're planning to start a family within a year or so. At the same time the other has their mind set on an inexpensive, economy compact that gets great gas mileage since the process of getting married and buying a new home has built up quite a debt load – not to mention your plans to have a child.

It is not likely that you'll be able to find one vehicle that perfectly satisfies both of you. You'll need to compromise. You already agree that you need a new car. A reasonable compromise may be to shop for a less expensive, smaller sized SUV that gets better than average gas mileage than most other SUV's, has a good safety track record and fewer bells and whistles. Both of you have compromised. Both of you had to let go of something you wanted in a new car while simultaneously you both got some of the things you wanted in a new car.

It should be mentioned that sometimes there are things that can not be compromised. If it's a matter of your core values or beliefs it is not likely that you'll be able to compromise. For instance, you may feel strongly about living near both of your families, especially as you begin planning to start your own. It wouldn't really matter if a new job opportunity opened up halfway across the country. No matter how much they tried to entice you, you wouldn't think about compromising and moving your family permanently away from all of your relatives.

The art and skill of compromise may come easier to some than others. There are some people who simply believe that they'd rather win at all costs rather than compromise (I hope you're not marrying a person who brings that philosophy into your marriage). If you are marrying a person with that philosophy or if that person is you, I hope that you're able to leave that side of yourself out in the street. While that attribute may make a person successful in some areas of life (or, so they think); it will make your marriage difficult, competitive, unfulfilling, and quite frankly, exhausting.

Pre-Marital Classes

Learning without thought is labor lost.

– Confucius

When you buy an appliance, it always comes with an instruction manual. When you buy clothing, it always comes with directions on how to clean it. Any electronic gadget you purchase will always come with an owner's manual or a user's manual. Do you see a pattern here?

One of the most important things that you'll do in life is get married and have a family. Yet, there is no instruction manual on how to do so. I suppose that means there is nothing to it. Ha! We wish!

Here are just some of the things we're supposed to instinctively know:

* We're supposed to innately know how to be in a good marriage.
* We're supposed to know what makes a good marriage work.
* We're supposed to know how to be the best spouse possible.
* We're supposed to know how to give support to one another as well as receive support from our spouse.
* We're supposed to be experts in communicating, loving, understanding, giving, supporting, nurturing, teaching, learning, respecting, listening, etc.

We have to go to school to earn a certificate, diploma, or degree in order to work in our chosen field. And even after we've been working in our chosen field, many of us still have to continue our education and training in order to earn a certificate or advanced degree in order to maintain our jobs and to qualify for promotions.

What requirements are necessary in order to get married? As far as training is concerned, absolutely none – there are no prerequisites to marriage. Again, this may be the single most important thing you do and yet there is no training required. You do need a marriage license and possibly blood tests in order to get married. But you don't have to study for a blood test! You simply have to fill out a form, pay the amount due, and you receive your license. There is no training required whatsoever.

Well, even if marriage training is not required, it can be very beneficial for the sake of your marriage to participate in premarital counseling. Some religions require that members take premarital counseling prior to being married. Although it may seem like an unnecessary hassle, it's excellent and very necessary!

You'll be given thorough training from a faith-based perspective. There are also non-faith-based organizations and institutions that provide premarital counseling. Either or both of these methods can provide valuable information that you could use on an everyday basis in your marriage. You may find that these classes are the difference between a marriage and a GREAT MARRIAGE!

Where would you find information on courses like this?

Look up:

1. relationship support classes
2. relationship skills

The following are a few links to helpful sites and articles that will guide you in finding the right form of premarital counseling for you:

a) http://www.couples-place.com/articles_advice/collections.asp
b) http://www.romancetips.com/marriage/newlyweds/honey-moonover.shtml
c) http://www.stayhitched.com/
d) http://www.washingtonpost.com/wp-dyn/content/article/2006/02/27/AR2006022701027.html?referrer=emailarticle

What do you learn in relationship courses? You'll learn things such as:

i. How to relate to one another.
ii. How to ensure past relationships do not influence your current relationship.
iii. How to nurture your relationship.
iv. How to communicate effectively.
v. How to ask for what you want.
vi. How to listen to your partner.
vii. How to resolve conflicts fairly.
viii. How to be intimate with your partner and the role intimacy plays in your marriage.
ix. How to negotiate and compromise.
x. How to have fun in your relationship.

Not all marital classes are designed to take months to complete and they aren't all in a group setting. There are several formats for these types of classes:

1. Home study

2. Internet
3. Books – Independent study
4. Seminars lasting from several hours to a day
5. Courses given over a couple of days to several months

In summary, invest in your future. Take the time and effort to establish good habits in relating towards one another. Learn effective ground rules, good communication skills, nurturing, forgiveness and patience. And remember, taking a premarital course or seminar is not a one-time event and does not indicate or suggest that there are problems in your relationship.

Developing a healthy relationship is an on-going lesson that you put into practice every day, week, month, and year "for as long as you both shall live." It is of utmost importance to get started on the right path and that's what a premarital course can provide; the tools to begin your journey together, as a couple, and to know how to work as a partnership.

It will be up to both of you to continue down this path by continuing to practice the lessons you've learned during your course. But it does not stop there. You can continue to take courses designed to enhance your relationship, and you must continue practicing the good lessons you learn. You will benefit immensely – it will be well worth it!

Your Reality

Few people have the imagination for reality.

– *Johann Wolfgang von Goethe*

*Y*our experiences during your upbringing are the greatest contributor to what your expectations will be when you get married. They shape your "reality" about what a family is and how it operates. To have a successful marriage, you'll have to understand that your reality is just a perception. It is your perception and it is very "real" to you, but it may or may not be the same reality that your mate has about being a spouse and having a family. For these reasons, it's important to talk about what you expect in your marriage BEFORE YOU GET MARRIED!

If your father washed the car while your mother prepared dinner every Sunday afternoon, that ritual may have become your expectation of what should happen in your own marriage. If on Sunday you prepare dinner, but your husband never washes the car, you may begin to feel as though "he never does anything right." Or, if you wash the car every Sunday and come inside and your wife hasn't even thought about cooking or asks you where you are going out to eat, you may start thinking "what's wrong with her?"

There is nothing wrong with your mate. He or she simply doesn't have the same "reality" as you, and your partner's expectations are different than your own.

Without talking about your upbringing, and more importantly, your expectations, your mate will never be able to know what you expect. That means he or she will never be able to meet your expectations.

The same is true in reverse. If your mate has certain expectations of what you should do, and doesn't share them with you, there is no way you'll be able to fulfill those expectations.

You must remember – there is no right or wrong. But, if you don't understand where your mate is coming from, and/or your partner doesn't understand where you're coming from, you could have problems or issues in this area.

When you understand each other's reality you'll be able to develop a new reality that merges or blends different aspects of each of your individual family experiences.

If one or both of you grew up in a single-parent household, it may be difficult to understand how a marriage can operate. You may have a dreamy, fantasy-like expectation of what a marriage would be like. Or, you may have a cynical outlook and expect failure and arguments to arise at every turn. Neither of those extremes is realistic and both can be devastating to building a good, solid relationship.

If one of you grew up as an only child in a single-parent household and the other grew up in a household where there were two parents, several children, grandparents, an aunt, three dogs and two cats, then you'll have lots of talking to do! You grew up in different worlds. There may have been similarities in some areas; for instance, both of you may have been fortunate enough to grow up in very loving homes. Or, both of you may have been less fortunate and grew up in homes where emotions were not expressed very well. You may have similar morals, and so on. You may have many similarities, but you have one major difference that very well was instrumental in shaping your "family reality."

If you've watched any of the popular "reality" television shows that portrays family lives where spouses exchange lives for a week or two, you'll realize that although lifestyles seem similar to the outside world, every family has their own way of doing things, their own rhythm and harmony and when mixed, those differences can become painfully clear. One of the biggest mistakes you can make in your marriage is to go in with blinders on and expect your "reality" to become your partners. It just doesn't work that way.

The best example of how a married couple relates to one another, whether it's a good example or a bad one, is the natural, everyday observation of your parents. If you are lucky to have parents who understand how to relate well to each other, who love, trust, respect, and communicate well with each other, then you have an intrinsically beautiful picture of how a good relationship works. No disrespect, but if you grew up in a household with two parents who did not understand how to relate, respect, or communicate well with one another, even though they may love each other as well as you very much, the example they set for you was not a good one - that is not to say that you can't learn from their mistakes, or learn on your own through hard work. The desire to understand how to relate well together and be the best partner you can must be present. It must be a conscious, ongoing effort if it is to work.

Now, for all of you who grew up in a household where your parents understood how to relate well with each other, just because you grew up in a household that was a good example, doesn't mean you don't have to work at being the best you can be, too. Granted, you had the opportunity to see on a daily basis how a good relationship looks. Since you had the good fortune to see how your parents work at relating to one another, many of the tools that are necessary in a good relationship may come more naturally to you. However, you too will have to work constantly on being the best you can be; it's not hereditary and you can't just expect that you'll choose the right path in each and every given situation.

There are millions of people who were raised in loving households that were headed by a single parent. However, people who were raised in this situation did not have the benefit of observing how a marital relationship works on a daily basis. Your "reality" of what a married relationship looks like is bound to be different than that of a person who grew up with two parents. The good news is you too will have to work hard towards being the best you can be in a relationship - just like everyone else.

Your reality vs. Your expectation

Your reality is what you understand a relationship should be, based upon your life experience. Your expectation is how you think you should be in a relationship and how you want your partner to be in your relationship. Are your expectations realistic? Do you think your husband should make a million dollars or more every year, buy you flowers every day, serenade you before every love making session, and be able to fix your car in the event it breaks down when you return home from your daily outing at the tennis club? Well, you may not have a realistic expectation of what marriage is all about.

Similarly, if you think your wife should greet you every day wearing varied sexy outfits at the front door when you come home from work, with dinner prepared and on the table, your bath drawn, and your clothes ironed and ready for you to wear tomorrow, well, you may be dreaming, clueless or both.

It's important that you know and understand what your expectations are and that your expectations are based in reality and not fantasy. It's equally important that your spouse understands your expectations and your expectations are consistent with your spouses'.

Remember, your expectations are not only what you expect from your mate, they are also what you expect to bring to the "marriage table." What do you expect to do for your mate when you're married? How do you expect that you'll relate and communicate with your mate? You should fully communicate your expectations and discuss any realistic ones before disappointment and/or resentment move into your home.

When an Only Child Gets Married

A man without a wife is like a vase without flowers.

– African Proverb

If you've cultivated a very close relationship with your parents, which only children sometimes do because they sometimes need more attention than a child who shares parents with other siblings, you'll want to include your parents in your new relationship, but not to the point where you drive your partner away.

Marriage is another stage of life and your parents hopefully will understand if you're not able to devote as much time to them as you have in the past. Enjoy this stage for its benefits and let your parents know that they're still needed, just not in the same way as when you were single.

If your fiancé is an only child, be patient and understanding as they cut the apron strings. Don't force the dissolution of his or her current relationship because that can only backfire in the end.

Here are a few online resources that will help you to understand the changes that are taking place and to share with the family who may be losing their only child to marriage:

* http://www.onlychild.com/currentissue/current.html
* http://amblesideonline.org/PR/PR12p609EducationOnlyChild.shtml
* http://www.onlychild.icom43.net/library.html

Common Things to Avoid

*My wife tells me she doesn't care what I do when I'm away,
as long as I'm not enjoying it.*

– Lee Trevino

We've discussed so many things that will help to strengthen your relationship. But there are things you can actively eliminate that will also strengthen your marriage. If you continue to practice these things, you run the risk of damaging the strong foundation on which you want your marriage to be built.

To build and maintain a strong relationship is a work in process. Learn to throw out all of the things that hurt your relationship and keep and continue to expand upon the things that will strengthen your relationship.

1. Don't hold grudges. You'll have a much better relationship if you learn to live and let go. Think about it…what does holding a grudge do for you and your relationship? How does it serve you? If something doesn't help your relationship, it hurts it – Period! It will serve you to let go of grudges. Holding a grudge wears on you. It makes you feel horrible. It's disruptive. It's negative. Think logically about it. Why would you want to hold onto something that's so negative?

   I was at a party several months ago and met a young woman who was engaged. She was at the party with her parents but her fiancé wasn't there because his flight had been severely delayed. She said, "I'll let it go this time but if we were married and he did this to me, I'd give him the silent treatment for at least a month."

   Whoa… I asked her, "First of all how is it his fault that his flight was delayed? And, even if he did something wrong, how would either of you benefit when you administered the silent treatment for a month?" It was like she was planning to be mean during their marriage - and he didn't even do anything wrong. She was sharpening up her grudge to use as a weapon for her unsuspecting soon-to-be-husband and their relationship.

Holding onto a grudge is a learned behavior. What you learn you can relearn or unlearn.

Learn to deal with disappointment in different ways that will serve you better. I'm not saying that whatever it is that's making you upset isn't important and doesn't need addressing. I'm saying that holding a grudge doesn't help to solve the root problem; it makes the situation worse, whatever it is.

Holding grudges is immature behavior. There! I said it. It's true. There are far better ways, more mature ways, to deal with things that are upsetting to you.

2. Bad habits. Those little every day annoyances have the potential to drive people crazy! You know what I'm talking about! It's funny; many times the one who does the annoying thing, and we all do them, actually knows about it. For instance, when you first start dating and everyone's on their best behavior, these annoying tendencies will never be seen by anyone. The person with the annoying habit will actually hide it, camouflage it, conceal it or mask it. They do this because they must know it's annoying or not proper. But after dating for a while, after living together or not long after marriage when you are both more comfortable with each other, these annoying habits will surface. If you know you have an annoying habit, pull it out by the root and whatever you did to get rid of it while dating, continue to do so throughout your marriage. I'm not suggesting that you should act phony or fake. I'm posing a question - if you know you do something that is annoying to your spouse, why would you purposely continue doing it?

Don't alienate your in-laws. Having a good relationship with your in-laws helps to build a strong family. Do you envision many holidays with all of your children around a huge dinner table along with both sets of parents? Those visions will be just that (a vision) if you don't strive to build a relationship with those who raised the one you love.

a) Be patient when dealing with the future in-laws.

b) Be understanding of his or her feelings, validate them, and communicate your own.

c) Never let things get to you. If your in-law grates on your nerves, leave the room. Don't stay in a situation where you may lose your cool and say something you'll later regret.

4. Whatever you do, never discuss your partner's bad habits with your parents. There are a few exceptions to this rule. If you have parents who aren't overly protective of you and won't jump to conclusions or hold things against your partner for the rest of his or her life, then it's okay to share your feelings with them on occasion. But BEWARE! You can't expect your parents to peacefully share the same dinner table with you and your spouse a year from now if they know your spouse did something to hurt you. It won't happen!

5. Don't allow your family to interfere in your relationship. Although you've listened to your parents and respected their advice up until now, once you're married, you become one with your spouse and if your family's advice is interfering with the plans for your marriage, it's time to cut the cord. Be respectful of your parents' feelings, but communicate to them that their interference is causing a disturbance in your marriage. You'd be surprised at how much they will understand. However, during your conversation, be sure that you're not placing blame on your spouse. This could cause a rift between your partner and your parents. Discuss the issues without blaming anyone and without insinuating that it's your spouse's idea to have less interference from your parents.

Lifestyles

Maturity is achieved when a person accepts life as full of tension.

– Joshua L. Liebman

Do you and your new spouse have compatible lifestyles? Many couples are able to work out discrepancies, but for some couples, this can be the source of discord.

- Busy Bee vs. Couch Potato – Is your spouse always on the go while you get tired just watching them run around trying to fit too many things into a single day? If this sounds familiar, there is no reason why your relationship has to suffer; simply come to an agreement that you don't have the energy or desire to do all of the things that he or she does. This works both ways. If you're the one who's constantly in motion while your spouse is quite comfortable relaxing seemingly all of the time to you – do not expect them to turn into a busy bee just because you're in their life now. You need to be true to yourself and so does your spouse. You don't have to change just because you're married to someone who doesn't approach life the same way as you. You don't have to become a busy bee if watching old movies in front of the fireplace is more up your alley. It's okay to be different. However, it is essential that you realize and understand that there are, indeed, differences between you and your mate. And more importantly, you must be willing to accept your mate the way he/she is. It took them a lifetime to become the way they are. It's not likely or reasonable to think that they will change their ways just because you're now in their life or because their lifestyle doesn't match yours.

- Hobbies - There are hobbies and interests that each of you has that may not interest your partner. Not only is that normal, it's healthy to have some interests, independent of your partner. One issue that many newlyweds face is how to retain your identity after you're married. After all, you were your own person before meeting your love. Now that you're married do you have to be just like your spouse? You don't. You'll do and experience many things together. (Some people say that if you're together long enough, you'll develop the same habits and speech patterns and some say that you'll even start looking alike.) However, it is beneficial to both of you to have interests and hobbies on your own.

- Identity – It's not a contradiction to also say that you'll retain some traits and identity that is yours and yours alone. This is healthy. Don't feel guilty if there are some things that you like to do and want to do that doesn't involve or interest your spouse. There will be some things that your spouse will like and want to do that you won't have any desire in doing. That's great!

- Balance - The key is balance. If you're constantly doing things that aren't of interest to your significant other, or if your spouse is constantly doing things without you – that's a problem. But if on an autumn weekend one of you wants to watch football all day long, and the other wants to go shopping, both of you should feel comfortable enjoying the things that make you happy. Neither of you should pressure the other into feeling guilty about what they like doing.

- On the go vs. Homebody – Do you dread shopping and running errands while your spouse spends more time in the car than at home? If you like to go and your spouse likes to stay, make a compromise so that you can do all the errands and shopping and allow your partner to be home, where he or she is happy, and vice versa. Communicate your feelings of needing to "get out" and understand if your spouse doesn't want to follow suit. Make a special day once a week or once a month when you can run errands together, but don't make it an all-day event. Be respectful of each other's wishes to be home or be gone and don't force the issue of "you never take me anywhere." Similarly, you can plan a special day once a month or so when both of you agree to stay at home and watch old movies all day long. Compromise and you'll find a common ground.

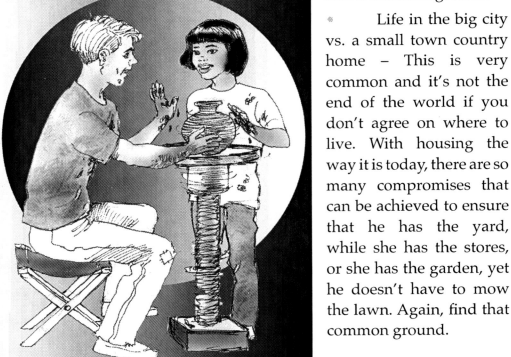

- Life in the big city vs. a small town country home – This is very common and it's not the end of the world if you don't agree on where to live. With housing the way it is today, there are so many compromises that can be achieved to ensure that he has the yard, while she has the stores, or she has the garden, yet he doesn't have to mow the lawn. Again, find that common ground.

Fun

Pleasure is the flower that passes; remembrance, the lasting perfume.

– Jean de Boufflers

What do you like to do for fun? Is it:

- Gardening,
- Investing,
- Dancing,
- Playing Cards,
- Traveling,
- Wine Tasting,
- Photojournalism,
- Reading,
- Watching Football,
- Playing golf,
- Volunteering,
- Boating/Fishing,
- Skiing,
- Shopping,
- Attending Horse/Auto Races,
- Concert Hopping,
- Computer gaming,
- Going to the Museum,
- Cultural Events,
- Fine Dining,
- Barbequing,

- Entertaining,
- Buying and Selling Houses,
- Hiking,
- Fishing,
- Playing computer games,
- Attending Seminars,
- Antiquing…?

It doesn't matter what you do, but it's important in a relationship to have some common interests. Sharing fun activities on a regular basis will strengthen your bond and your relationship in so many ways:

- You want to support one another by having fun and having an outlet that you can share and share alike.
- You'll spend unforced time together.
- You'll be able to communicate in a common language.
- Similar things and events will excite you.

When you think of it, having fun together was probably one of the first things that drew you together in the first place. Arguably, the definition of dating is doing things together and having fun while learning about each other. When we get married, our life changes in many ways. Suddenly, our main focus isn't about having fun. Responsibility sets in and as a result we too often forget to have fun or it seems as though it is not such a priority. Please do not fall into this trap. Couples who make fun an integral part of their married lives stand a much better chance of developing, enjoying and sustaining a successful marriage. If having fun together comes naturally – great! If having fun does not come naturally or if your responsibilities seem to have you bogged down, then make a point to schedule time for fun activities. Hmmmm… that sounds like dating all over again. Just because you're married does not mean you can't still date each other. Actually, going on "dates" regularly with your spouse is very invigorating and healthy for your relationship. And, it's fun!

Ten Steps to a Healthy Marriage

Love does not consist of gazing at each other,
but in looking together in the same direction.

– Antoine de Saint-Exupery

$\mathcal{H}$ealthy marriages are built of many small blocks that create a firm footing, but there are ten key things to remember when building your perfect marriage. Work toward achieving these ten things, and there will be very little you won't be able to overcome:

1. Love
2. Communication
3. Understanding
4. Patience
5. Forgiveness
6. Acceptance
7. Trust
8. Fun
9. Compromise
10. Intimacy

(Does order matter? Have fun and prioritize this list in the order that is most relevant to you. Ask your partner to do the same. Then compare both lists. This might reveal some interesting and important things about both of you!)

Questions to Ask Before Taking the Leap

1. To what kind of family structure are you accustomed?

2. Are your lifestyles compatible?

3. Do you have honest, open communication?

4. Is your relationship based on the theory "opposites attract" or are you "two peas in a pod?"

5. Are you comfortable "being yourself" in the presence of your fiancé/spouse?

6. Do you consider you and your fiancé/spouse the best of friends?

7. Do you hold any resentment, hostility, envy, jealousy or harbor any ill feelings towards your fiancé/spouse?

8. If your fiancé/spouse communicated to you that something you do simply "gets on their nerves," what would you do?

9. Is everything perfect about your relationship?

   a) Are you looking at your relationship through rose colored glasses?

   b) Is your assessment fair, honest and accurate?

10. Do you handle disagreements constructively?

**Notes, thoughts, ideas,
questions and issues I want to
discuss with my love...**

Chapter Thirteen

Intimacy

Trip over love, you can get up. Fall in love and you fall forever.

– Author Unknown

Intimacy - The condition or feeling of being close and belonging together.

– Reginald Wickham

Intimacy in marriage is the glue that holds it together. It's not an end, but a means. It's a process; a progression. It's a way to be. It's to be practiced and developed. Intimacy grows deeper and stronger as your relationship grows, and vise versa. It, however, must be actively practiced. If intimacy is left alone, it will ultimately deteriorate and weaken your relationship.

Some people immediately equate intimacy and sex, while others see intimacy as emotional caring, sharing and communicating. Oftentimes, it's perceived to be split or divided along gender lines, with men being the ones who equate intimacy and sex and women being the ones who think of intimacy in terms of emotional sharing and communicating. These perceptions may be true, or they may be a myth.

Intimacy can and probably will look different for each couple. What one couple describes as intimacy may be different than another's description.

Sex and intimacy are not equal. But sex is a very important component in intimacy, and just because I'm saying it's not equivalent does not and should not diminish the importance of a healthy, fulfilling, fun, mutually satisfying, pleasurable, passionate, and safe sexual relationship.

In any case, "Intimacy" encompasses sex and communication, as well as so much more...

The truth of the matter is that intimacy has many components:

- Intimacy is moments in time shared together, and comes in the form of emotional intimacy, intellectual intimacy, sensual or sexual intimacy, and spiritual intimacy.

- Intimacy is a deep understanding of each other.

- Intimacy is bonding.

- Intimacy is companionship.

- Intimacy is friendship.

- Intimacy is love.
- Intimacy is being vulnerable.
- Intimacy is trust.
- Intimacy is communicating on various levels.
- Intimacy is sex.
- Intimacy is saying something without saying anything.
- Intimacy is passion.
- Intimacy is knowing and caring about what pleases each other.
- Intimacy is that special look or that special smile shared between you and you alone.
- You can experience intimacy when working together towards a common goal.
- You can experience intimacy when listening to music at a concert or in your living room.
- You can experience intimacy in absolute silence.
- You can experience intimacy by riding bikes together, playing golf, gardening, or skiing together.

- You can even experience intimacy, believe it or not, while going through or experiencing an emergency or dealing with a problem – together.

This list is not at all conclusive, but instead, illustrates that intimacy is not one dimensional. Here are some tips to keep the intimacy alive and burning in your marriage:

- Say "I love you" at least once a day.
- Write love notes and leave them in unexpected places.
- Have fun and keep your relationship "young and light-hearted."
- Call your spouse "pet" names.
- Make time for sexual intimacy on a regular basis, no matter how tired you are or how bad your head hurts.
- Share meals together as often as possible.
- Share special times together. When you don't have time to share – Make time!
- Don't expect every sexual encounter to be "magic" with fireworks.
- If the fireworks seem to be gone, work toward rekindling the flame. Try something different, new and exciting.
- Be responsive to your partner's needs. Sex isn't one-sided and if your partner isn't feeling fulfilled, he or she may not be in the mood the next time you are.

Expressing intimacy can include:

- Touching
- Talking
- Sharing
- Kissing
- Caring
- Holding hands
- Playing footsy

- Looking into each other's eyes
- Kissing again
- Fondling
- Being affectionate
- Romancing
- Kissing some more
- Going on a picnic

Intimacy can be shared while physically touching or without touching at all. A game was described to me where a couple sits or lies, facing each other. The couple talks to each other while getting closer and closer and talking softer and softer. The rules are you can talk about whatever you like…goals for the future, plans for an upcoming romantic vacation, making love, your favorite experience, your fantasies, a secret that you have yet to reveal. As you share, according to the rules of this game, you talk softer and softer and look into each other's eyes while getting closer and closer – without actually touching. You can stop talking if you'd like. You can close your eyes if you'd like. Feel the heat of your bodies so very close to each other.

Play this "game" for as long a period as you'd like and as often as you'd like.

Have fun! In this game both of you are winners. What matters most is how you play the game.

A variation of this game is what I call "virtual massaging." Set the mood. Turn down the lights. Light some candles. Have your favorite music playing softly in the background. Open a bottle of wine.

Have the one receiving the "virtual massage" lie down while the "virtual masseuse" uses his or her hands, and any other body part, hovering over as close to your body as possible with loving, gentle strokes, but without actually touching bodies.

You can play this game clothed or unclothed. Or you can disrobe slowly, one article of clothing at a time, just prior to that body part being "virtually massaged."

According to the rules, if you are the masseuse and you actually touch your partner, you lose. Or, if you're being massaged and you move purposely, brushing your partner, you lose. But, as mentioned before, no one actually loses.

I guarantee these are win-win games.

Take turns giving and receiving virtual massages.

After your virtual massages, you may want to give and receive real massages with oils, powders and fragrances and…Well, you get the idea! Use your imagination and creativity.

Make up your own games.

If nurtured and practiced regularly, intimacy grows stronger and deeper as time goes on.

"As intimacy grows, so grows your relationship!" - R. Wickham

It really doesn't get old. It only gets better over time.

And, intimacy does not go away or disappear for older or aging couples. Intimacy won't look the same for a newlywed couple as it does for a couple who's been married for 20 years. It shouldn't. If it does, that would mean that as a couple you haven't grown at all in 20 years.

Enjoy time together as often as you can. Time spent together, no matter what you're doing, can be very intimate.

You can be intimate when the two of you are alone, you can share intimacy with a handful of other people present, or in a crowd of thousands. Take a moment and steal a glance, a wink, a gentle touch, a squeeze, a warm smile or a whisper. Even if you're on a crowded city bus during rush hour or in the middle of a packed stadium, your intimate gestures and expressions will be heartfelt -- and returned. The more you give the more you get. It's one of those laws of the universe. Keep practicing the art of intimacy. It's a beautiful thing. It won't get old - it rejuvenates and keeps you excited about your marriage!

Also, don't let children wipe out your intimacy. Many couples fall into this unfortunate trap. Continue expressing intimacy whether your children are in your presence or not. Talk, share, touch, laugh, wink, hold hands, kiss, smile, and love each other right there in front of your children. When they are in your presence, no matter what their ages, they'll be learning a valuable lesson of how to relate to a partner and how a great relationship works.

The following are some links to articles and sites that give great information and tips to keep your intimacy alive:

- http://www.christianitytoday.com/mp/2006/002/18.20.html - Tips to understanding the unrealistic expectations of marital intimacy, both sexual and non-sexual. ALSO a free subscription to magazine, Marriage Partnership.
- http://marriage.about.com/od/tips/qt/happymarriage.htm
- http://www.themarriagebed.com/
- http://www.foreverfamilies.net/xml/articles/marital_intimacy.aspx

Questions to Ask Before Taking the Leap

1. Do you have the same ideas of intimacy as your partner?

2. Do you share a strong intimate bond now?

3. How would you change your intimate moments?

4. Is your partner the intimate type who will fulfill your emotional needs throughout the life of your marriage?

5. Have you seen or felt signs that the level of intimacy in your relationship changes or grows?

6. Do you and your fiancé/spouse find it easy to be intimate with each other?

7. Does being intimate come easy or natural for you or do you have to force yourself or work hard at it?

8. When your partner is being intimate with you do you feel comfortable?

9. Do you feel that your partner is ever too intimate?

10. Have you ever or would you ever use intimacy as a "weapon" by purposely holding back?

11. Have you ever or would you ever use intimacy as currency by being extra intimate in order to get your way by bribing your fiancé/spouse?

Notes, thoughts, ideas, questions and issues I want to discuss with my love...

Chapter Fourteen

Family Matters

An ounce of blood is worth more than a pound of friendship.

– Spanish Proverb

*Y*ou are about to become a member of someone else's family. Your fiancé is about to become a member of yours. And both of you are starting a brand new family - together.

How well do you know your fiancé's family? Have you met his or her parents? Do you have any type of relationship with them? Do you live nearby, perhaps in the same town or a neighboring community? Do you live within a few hours of them? Do you live in the same time zone? Do you live in the same country? How about your fiancé's siblings and their families? Do you know them and do you have a relationship with them? Does your fiancé have any children? Do they live together or do the children live apart from your fiancé? Have you met your fiancé's children? Do you have a good relationship with them? Is the mother or father of your fiancé's children in your fiancé's life? How would you describe their relationship? Have you met them? What kind of relationship do you have with your fiancé's children's other parent(s)?

Getting to know the family members of your fiancé is beneficial in many ways. In most cases, showing a genuine interest in knowing the members of your fiancé's family and allowing them to get to know you show that you are open, willing, and looking forward to becoming the newest member of their family.

It would be ideal if you got along with everyone in his or her family and everyone liked and got along with you. That is possible and it is the best case scenario, but it doesn't always work that way.

If you don't get along with anyone in your fiancé's family and none of them get along with you…Hmmmm…That's an unusual situation – one that you probably need to examine very closely before you two jump the broom!

The most likely situation is that you'll get along with most members of your new family, but there may be one or a couple of members that no matter how hard you try, you just don't seem to be able to connect with them.

Keep trying, don't quit. Keep extending the olive branch without doing anything that compromises you or your values and integrity. Chances are, that person doesn't get along with many other people and is likely to have issues and or demons he or she has to battle and you just happen to be on the receiving end of their wrath.

The rest of the family is probably no stranger to the behavior and attitudes of that family member and will recognize and admire you for "fighting the good fight." Your fiancé will probably be the one most appreciative of your efforts.

This situation will be played in reverse, too. Your spouse-to-be will meet and have to learn to relate to your family as well. Are your parents living? Do they live near where you and your spouse are planning to make your home? Do you have siblings? Do you have any offspring?

All of these family members, not to mention aunts, uncles, cousins, in-laws, and the rest of your entire family, will be meeting and developing a relationship with the new addition to your family – the person with whom you chose to share the rest of your life -the person you chose to marry.

What would you do or how would you feel if your fiancé didn't want to be around your family? What would you do or how would you feel if your family didn't like your fiancé and acted rude, closed, obnoxious, mean, unkind, cruel, or malicious towards your honey? You would probably be devastated. After all, you probably wish that the people who mean most to you, namely your fiancé and your entire family, got along together. If they clearly don't like each other, that will bring stress upon you and everyone else involved.

Is there a way, through good communication and good effort on the part of all involved, to remedy the situation? Perhaps your fiancé and the rest of your family initially got off to a bad start when they first met or knew of one another. Is it possible that you contributed to the bad start of their relationship(s)? For instance, did you hide your fiancé from your family? Did you misrepresent your fiancé in any way? Did you share something your partner did that would cause your family to distrust his or her intentions toward you?

Knowing and understanding the source of the bad relations between your fiancé and the rest of your family is, or can be very helpful in determining how to best resolve their relationship going forward.

The main thing is for all parties to be able to put to rest their previous concerns and other roadblocks that are damaging to their relationship. They will each have to commit to starting over. If your fiancé and/or the members of your family are unwilling, or do not want to do the necessary work to begin a new, good, and strong relationship with each other, it will cause stress on you and every one else involved.

You may be able to facilitate the process by speaking to each member of your family and to your fiancé individually prior to having everyone get together. Communicate how much you love each other and give examples to demonstrate how you care for each other. Share some, but not necessarily all of the plans that you are making together for your future. This is meant to have your family understand that the two of you are serious about your relationship and committed and devoted to building a great union together.

You shouldn't feel as though you are reporting to your family, but they may have questions and as long as they're not being too nosy or intrusive, it probably would be helpful if their questions were answered.

What kinds of questions are appropriate? It may help if you're able to take a step back and ask yourself, "If I were in their shoes, would I have similar questions?" Or, "When 'so and so' got engaged, did they share with me the same kind of information my family is now asking of me?" Or, "What value is it to ignore their question or refuse to answer it? Or deeper still, what am I hiding?"

You know your family better than anyone. If you feel your family may be stepping over the line, ask yourself these questions:

* Is my family always this inquisitive?
* Am I usually this guarded or protective?
* Is this situation typical, or is it out of the ordinary?
* What do I think is the source of all of the questions from my family?

You may want to be frank with your family, "I don't understand what all of the questions about my fiancé are about." Perhaps if you understood where they were coming from, it would be easier to understand their motivation, and therefore, it would assist you in providing answers to their questions.

When a family member or close friend shares that they are getting married, it's a normal response for family and friends to ask questions about the new person who is about to become your spouse. So, you may want to look deep within yourself to understand why you're feeling that you don't need to, or shouldn't have to answer any questions about your mate.

Children

Kids: they dance before they learn there is anything that isn't music.

– William Stafford

Are you planning to have children? Before you get married, a major topic of discussion is whether both of you are on the same page regarding parenting. It's not important what you decide as a couple, as long as you're in agreement. If you assume that your fiancé and you share the same desires regarding parenting, yet you actually have differing opinions, the subject of children could be very difficult to resolve.

If you don't want children, for whatever reason, you must be honest and relate this to your partner. Similarly, if you want children, for whatever reason, you must relate this to your partner. Be honest with your feelings on the subject of children. Your marriage will have no possible future if one of you wants to be a parent and the other wants to travel and have fun as a childless couple. It's better to find out before you take the leap that you have differing views than one, two, or five years down the road.

Another topic of discussion should be, "How many children do we want?" If both of you want one child – cool. If both of you want nine or ten children – great! In other words, whether both of you want the same type of family, big or small – that's wonderful. You're both on the same page.

The difficulty arises when each of you has a different idea of what size of family you'd like to have. If one of you truly wants at least five or six children and the other only wants one, you have a huge discrepancy in the type of family you'll have. By today's standards, one of you wants a small family while the other wants a fairly large family.

Neither of you are right or wrong. It's not at all a question of being right or wrong. It's just that your idea of a family is not the same. That's all.

Perhaps one of you grew up in a large family, so that's what you're accustomed to, that's what you know, and that's what you want, while your partner may have been raised in a small family. Maybe they were an only child. Therefore, that's what they know and hence, that's what they want. Or maybe because you grew up as an only child you always wished for a large family when you got married. It doesn't really matter.

What matters is these types of issues should be discussed before you get married. These are the types of things that, if left un-discussed prior to getting married, could potentially be a difficult topic to start discussing after you're married, to say the least. If they are left unresolved, they can be very destructive to your relationship.

Planned Parenting

Give me the life of the boy whose mother is nurse, seamstress,
washerwoman, cook, teacher, angel, and saint, all in one,
and whose father is guide, exemplar, and friend. No servants
to come between. These are the boys who are born to the best fortune.

– Andrew Carnegie

To have children is a blessing in any way that they enter your life. Would you prefer such a life-changing event be a planned process? Or would you rather have this life-changing event be a total, unplanned, unthought-of surprise?

Another way of thinking about it is would you like to be physically, emotionally and financially prepared when you bring a new life into this world? Or do you want to have this life-changing event occur when you're totally unprepared?

You have several options regarding birth control methods such that except in a very minute number of cases you can prevent unwanted pregnancies with startling degrees of accuracy. This means when you're ready to have a family, or add to your family by having a child, you can similarly do so with a certain degree of assuredness and conviction.

It takes discipline to stick to a birth control regiment. But consider this…

- The next time you're in a grocery store, walk down the baby aisle and look at the price of disposable diapers, formula, milk, baby shampoo, and baby wipes, etc.

- Think about how much baby clothes cost.

- Shop around for a baby crib, bassinette, high chair, and car seat.

- Research what the difference would be in your out-of-pocket expenses if you increased your medical coverage from the employee & spouse plan to the family plan.

- Consider the co-pay amounts that you'd be responsible for each time you take your child for a visit to the doctor.

- Consider the costs for day care, private school, and moving to a larger home.
- Then consider how much you'd have to save each year over the next 18 years to send a child to college.

After you tally all of that, multiply it by at least two to take into account all of the things you forgot. Then add some more for the newest, latest and greatest things that you are not even aware of that you'll absolutely have to have!

Then take a walk down the health and beauty aisle or see your doctor and price various birth control methods.

Compare the two amounts, and make a choice. Would you rather spend a little on birth control, or would you prefer to take a chance on pregnancy, effectively playing Russian roulette while having unprotected sex with your spouse?

It's a choice. It's your choice.

If your religious affiliation determines that you can't use contraception, then you'll have to be extra careful. There are certain times during a monthly cycle when pregnancies are more likely than others. During these times, you'll have to use your brain and abstain from sex, or modify your sexual practices refraining from intercourse if your desire is to not have children at this time.

Get all of the information you can to help you with this most important decision. Local Planned Parenthood sites and various healthcare agencies have tons of information for couples who want to wait before they have a child. Usually, the information is discounted or free. Be informed before you change your lives forever.

Having children is one of the most universally loving, fundamental expressions of a marriage. In fact, there are many who say that bearing children is the primary role of the union of matrimony.

However, it's obviously not a requirement. If you don't choose to have children, don't let the pressure of society, your family, your religion, your friends, your co-workers or anyone else force you into doing something that you really don't want to do.

You two must decide whether or not you want children. This is an extremely important decision; one that will be with you for the rest of your lives.

Since this is such an important decision, challenge yourselves by asking, "Why do we want a child or children?" If you can't answer this question, or if the only answer you can come up with is, "Because everyone else is having children," or "because I like the smell of a baby," maybe you should wait a while before you have a child.

Many people have children for selfish reasons. Some people have children because they want to dress up the cute babies. Some people want their child to play sports or enter modeling contests, and desire to live vicariously through their children. Some couples decide to have a child in an attempt to make their troubled relationship better.

Having children is arguably the single most important decision you'll ever make. No one can stop you from having children for the wrong reasons, but it's best for everyone involved – especially the child – if you have his or her best interests in mind when you make this extremely important decision.

Many children are conceived when they've not been planned. Certainly, there are a very small percentage of cases when you're using birth control and there is simply a malfunction or an accident. There is nothing you can do about that. It's rare, but it does happen occasionally.

But what happens more often is that no birth control is used, or it's used incorrectly. More times than not, an unplanned pregnancy is the result of no contraception at all – the incorrect use or application of contraception methods - or the fact that you forgot (purposely or otherwise) to take or apply your birth control.

You can get instructions on how to properly use whatever method of birth control you choose from a few sources, including your physician or an agency such as Planned Parenthood. You should consider these avenues before there is an unwanted or unexpected pregnancy.

If you're not ready to have a child and you're having unprotected sex, you're really just asking for trouble. In this case, if your actions result in a pregnancy, that's not a mistake. That's a bad choice. You chose to have unprotected sex and, quite naturally, it resulted in a pregnancy.

Many times an unwanted pregnancy results in a beautiful baby and many parents say it's the best thing that ever happened to them. Well, that's a happy ending to an uncertain beginning.

I'm going to be frank and say, don't let the rest of your life be shaped by a bad choice. Having a baby is a beautiful thing. Having a baby when the baby is born to parents who planned for the pregnancy is even more beautiful.

She's Having a Baby

Now the thing about having a baby —
and I can't be the first person to have noticed this -
is that thereafter you have it.

– Jean Kerr

Prepare for the arrival of your newborn as much as you possibly can. Although there is no way to know everything that you'll need to know, you can help yourself and your baby by learning and familiarizing yourself with as much information about child birth and child care. Attend prenatal classes, read books and magazines, and talk to those who already have families.

The dynamics of your household will forever change when you have children. If you don't already have children, and you decide to have your first child, the difference in your daily lives from having no children to having a child will be extremely dramatic. You'll be responsible for a little human being; a person who will be dependent on you for everything.

Whether this is your first child, or you already have children, you can benefit by taking parenting classes. Also, no matter what stage your child is in, whether you have a newborn, toddler, youngster, or teen, there is a wealth of information available to help you and your child navigate through each phase they'll go through.

Parenting classes will offer insight to nutrition and breast feeding, the growth and development of your child, safety, first aid, potty training and medical concerns regarding young children.

You'll need other skills as well such as patience, understanding, discipline and dealing with stress and frustration (Oh that's right…Your baby will be perfect and you won't have any stress or frustration!)

Educate yourselves on what to expect throughout the pregnancy. Learn what changes are likely to take place in your marriage. Understand your new roles as lovers once there are three or more in your household. And gain as much knowledge on how to properly raise your child and give them as many opportunities to become the best they can be.

Children don't come with instruction booklets and you're not going to be perfect parents. You may not know exactly what to do in the beginning; just relax, take the best possible care of your child that you can. Give them love in abundance. Teach them the very best you can. And look for advice from those who have successfully raised incredible children; i.e. your parents.

Children From Previous Relationships

Children begin by loving their parents; as they grow older
they judge them; sometimes they forgive them.

– Oscar Wilde

oes either or both of you have children from previous marriages or relationships? If so, you'll need to discuss the ramifications of your new family structure.

Will children from your previous relationship live with you? Has the other parent, the one who is not a part of this marriage, given up parental rights? Will the spouse-to-be who is not the biological parent to this child formally adopt this child or these children once you get married? How will the biological parent feel if your new spouse disciplines the child? If both of you have children from previous relationships, do they all get along? Are their ages close together, or are there huge gaps? If your children aren't going to live with you, is one of you still responsible for child support payments? How will that affect your new family's budget and finances? How will your visitation rights blend in with your new married family? Do your ex-partner and your fiancé get along? They'll likely have to see one another, communicate with one another or, hopefully, at least be cordial to one another.

These are major issues that must be discussed prior to tying the knot. Many arrangements and considerations have to be planned in the best interest of the child or children involved. That is the fact that should never be overlooked. The adults in this situation must act like adults; as difficult as the situation may be. And, the child's or children's best interest must be paramount.

Okay, in the event that all children from previous relationships will be living with you under one household, there must be equality in how you raise both sets of children (And, your children if you have any children together!) You simply can't treat one set of children differently than the way you treat the others. Children are very intelligent, intuitive, and observant. They'll absolutely be able to detect whether or not they're being treated fairly.

As a matter of fact, even if you believe they're being treated fairly, they may perceive that they're being treated unfairly. This is not uncommon, and you'll have to be extremely sensitive and aware of your children's behavior, demeanor, attitude, performance in school, eating habits, etc. to pick up on any clues that there may be a problem.

Sometimes you'll be able to handle the problem or situation on your own by talking to the child and letting him or her express their feelings. Sometimes, their teachers or guidance counselors will be able to intervene and help. And if the child and the rest of your family need the help and assistance of professionals – so be it. You must do any and everything that you can, as soon as you identify that there is a problem for the benefit of your child.

The rest of your child's life depends on it.

If one or both of you will still be responsible for child support, you'll have to consider this as an ongoing expense when you're figuring out your family budget.

(See Chapter Four)

This can have a major impact on your income, and it must be known ahead of time and planned and prepared for. Ignoring it or hiding it from your significant other until after the wedding is nothing short of cruel.

There may be legal issues that need to be addressed regarding children from previous marriages or relationships. Adoption, child support, visitation, etc. are examples of why you'll need to consult a family law attorney. Consulting the attorney prior to getting married may be beneficial. The attorney will be working in your best interest and in the best interest of the child. There may be some things that you can or should do before getting married that may help out your situation.

If you contact your attorney after you're already married, these options may not be applicable any more. If you contact your attorney before getting married and there is really nothing that you can do to better your situation, your attorney will let you know. But, it's better that you ask before you get married, just in case.

"My Children" vs. "Your Kids"

There is only one pretty child in the world, and every mother has it.

– Chinese Proverb

*C*an you love your child too much? Of course not! That was a trick question. But the possibility of devoting too much time, attention, care, and love to your child, which results in one or both of you not having enough time to devote to each another, exists.

Your relationship as a married couple is now and will always be your primary relationship. Your child is, as most will agree, "the best thing that ever happened to you." However, never let your feelings of love for your child overshadow that of your partner in life.

When one of you has a child from a previous relationship, and subsequently, you meet, fall in love, and ultimately marry, this dynamic is more and more common. After all, you knew your child and established a beautiful bond well before you even met your new spouse.

But, no spouse wants to feel like they're second to anyone, including your child. Depending on the spouse you choose, this could even cause resentment and jealousy.

On the other hand, your child has been with you literally forever, from his or her prospective. Now, here comes a person in your life that you've fallen in love with and you're devoting so much time, attention, energy, and love towards them. Your children may see this as time, energy, and love that used to be theirs and may feel anxious, jealous, angry, confused and frustrated due to this new development.

Your child should not be made to feel any less worthy of your love and may need extra care and attention as you and your significant other develop your relationship.

Huh?

On one hand your partner needs your time and attention, and on the other hand your child needs your love and attention, more than ever before. How is one to deal with all of that?

It's not an easy balancing act, to say the least. You and your partner are adults, and should be able to understand and effectively communicate your needs and concerns. If you need help – GET IT.

Your child, on the other hand, may not be able to quite understand the feelings that accompany this new dynamic in a changing family life. Although he or she may be quite happy that you've found someone to love and cherish, they may have other feelings of fear, jealousy, anger, and resentment which can be very confusing to a young mind. Your children may be well served by getting counseling and any other help they need during this period of transition.

It may be a great thing for all involved to do things together as a family; the two who fell in love and have decided to marry and live the rest of their lives together, as well as each child that either of you have had together or from former relationships. All of the interpersonal relationships in this new "blended" family may need a little guidance, leadership and direction from the adults, especially at first. But try to let these relationships develop as naturally as possible.

Adoption

Children are one third of our population and all of our future.

– Select Panel for the Promotion of Child Health, 1981

To adopt a child is an act of angels. There are thousands of children who need a loving, caring and supportive, safe home. Whatever the reason you may be considering adoption, there is a great need for parents like you!

Of course, you'll need to discuss the possibility of adoption together. This is something that may or may not come up before you get married. If you agree that you want children, but for whatever reason you can't have children, many couples look to adoption as a remedy to fulfill their parenting needs. Whether you have children of your own or not this is a great option or alternative. And, you may not even think of it being a possibility until you've been married for many years.

The adoption process can be a very long and arduous one, but it can be worth every trying moment.

Adoption can hit your family in another way, too.

If you experience an unplanned pregnancy, what are you going to do? One option is to keep the baby – even though you didn't plan for it. You may decide that you want to keep and nurture this beautiful baby born to you.

Another option is to abort the pregnancy. This is a very difficult decision to make. Both of you should be in accord with this decision – as you should with any decision regarding any pregnancy in your relationship. And yet another option is to put the baby up for adoption. This too is a very hard decision. But although difficult, it potentially can be the best, most loving decision you can make in the best interest of your baby.

If you're considering adopting a baby, you'll need to consider:

- Domestic vs. international adoption
- Same race vs. different race adoptions
- Sex of the child

- Age of the child
- Cost of adoption
- Open or closed adoption
- Will you know the health history of your baby?

If you're considering giving your baby up for adoption, you'll need to consider:

- Do you want to know the family who adopts your child?
- Do you want to be anonymous?
- Will you be prepared to handle birthmother's grief if and when it occurs?

Educate yourself on all of your options before you commit to a decision you may later regret. There is a ton of information about adoption from a variety of sources. One helpful site is http://adoptionnetwork.com/adoptiveparents/?gcid=C13083X068. There are many other great sites that can answer any questions you may have about your options. Check out as many sources as possible in your search.

Schools

You send your child to the schoolmaster,
but 'tis the schoolboys who educate him.

– Ralph Waldo Emerson

What kind of school will your children attend? Will they attend public school, private school, parochial school, boarding school, or be home-schooled? Where you live may determine where your child goes to school. Or the opposite or inverse of that statement may be true. Where you want your child to go to school may determine where you decide to live.

Thus, schooling may have a significant input when you and your partner are determining where to move, live and make your home. If you don't have children yet, and are not planning to have them for a significant amount of time, then schools will probably not be a factor when you're considering where you want to live.

But if you already have children, or are considering starting a family in a relatively short period of time, schooling may be one of the most important aspects in determining where you and your family will reside.

A growing trend these days is home-schooling. If you and your partner feel strongly about this, home-schooling may be an option for you.

Check with your local and state government to find out what schooling options you have and do your homework to find the best schools for your children. Realize that each individual child will be different in his or her particular educational needs, and what works for one may not work for the other. If your child is gifted in a particular area or has special needs, you'll have to consider that as well, as you research the best educational options for your child. If you keep this in mind and do what's best for your child and his or her education, you'll make the right decision.

The following are a few helpful sites and articles that can aid you in your search for the right education for your child. (Please note some of these websites may represent a particular geographical area not in close proximity to where you live. However, it is still important to understand the type of information available. You may look for similar information available in your neck of the woods).

- Education for the gifted child - some do's and don'ts to keep in mind - http://www.educationaloptions.com/raising_gifted_ children.htm

- Private School option - http://www.wright-house.com/ac/ papers97/Wang-education.html

  - Managing tuition costs for private school - http://privateschool. about.com/od/financing/qt/tuitionfees.htm?terms=private+ education+loans

- An Education for children with special needs -

  - Autism - http://autism.about.com/od/schoolandsummer/a/ edoptionshub.htm

  - Learning and Attention deficits - http://www. educationalconnections.com/services.htm#childrenlearning

  - Deaf or Hard of Hearing - http://www.entnet.org/healthinfo/ hearing/hearing_loss_communication.cfm

  - http://www.ed.gov/about/offices/list/osers/products/ opening_doors/index.html

- Home school option -

  - Grandmother is concerned about the grandchild's success if home schooled - http://homeschooling.about.com/

  - Suggested course of study for traditional schools could help with home schooling, helps understand how to categorize your child's educational needs - http://homeschooling.about.com/ cs/learning/a/courseofstudy.htm

  - Research institute which studies home schooling - http://www. nheri.org/

  - HSLDA is available for legal advice. www.hslda.org

- Trend toward sending children to Charter School –

- Frequently asked questions (FAQs) about charter schools - http://www.mainecharterschools.org/ABCs%20of%20Charter%20Schools/Key%20Features.htm
- What are Charter schools and what do parents need to know? http://www.psparents.net/CharterSchools.htm
- PUBLIC schools - the good side - http://www.osba.org/commsvcs/natfacts.htm
- Challenging "misinformation" about public schools - http://www.osba.org/commsvcs/challeng.htm

Discipline

My mom used to say it doesn't matter how many kids you have...
because one kid'll take up 100% of your time, so more kids
can't possibly take up more than 100% of your time

– Karen Brown

A normal and required part of parenting is disciplining your child. Every child, no matter how good you say they are, needs discipline once in a while. Some children need it more than others.

There are many ways in which to discipline a child. There are many different styles of discipline. Some are approved methods, while others are not. Some are old-fashioned, while many new methods of discipline are developed and taught. And you may develop your own methods of disciplining your child.

You'll probably utilize a few different styles of discipline; discovering what works best for the individual child and you may change styles depending on the phase your child is going through.

If you have more than one child, you may very likely find that one style of discipline is effective for one child, while another style of discipline is more effective for your other child.

One crucial aspect of disciplining your child or children is that you, as a couple, must be on the same page. Not only is it not effective if your styles are vastly different and non-complementary, it's also very confusing to your child and will cause further problems.

Your children's behavior is a window to what's going on in their lives. Children have yet to fully develop the skills needed to understand what may be bothering them and how to express or communicate it. So they may act out in ways that are not typical for their behavior.

You'll have to be keenly aware of sudden differences in behavior as clues that they may be experiencing difficulties that they can't quite articulate.

When you discipline your children you must remember that you're their parent; not their best friend. They have school mates, siblings, and peers that will and should be their best friends. You have a spouse, friends, co-workers, peers, and/or siblings who you should look to when you need a friend. You'll love your child more than anyone else on the planet, but to serve them best, remember; they're not your friend. They are your children. The parent – child relationship is very unique. It's a very different dynamic; a very different type of relationship.

Some parents think they're being mean or too harsh when discipline is in order. Some parents choose not to discipline their children because they think their child won't like them as much. Other parents don't discipline their children, saying and/or believing that the child is simply expressing himself or herself and the parent doesn't want to inhibit that expression.

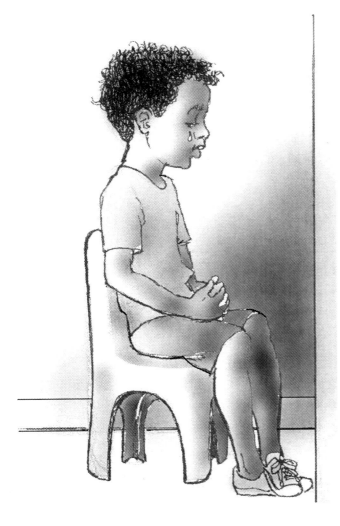

These feelings, albeit somewhat normal and understandable, are really worse for your child. Children need discipline. They actually crave it. They need for their parents to set limits and boundaries. Children naturally may challenge the limitations you set. That's their "job" as children. They need for their parents to be adults and do their jobs by applying appropriate discipline when these boundaries and limits are challenged and crossed.

Many people say, "…little children, little problems; big children, big problems!"

It's easier to discipline a young child and continue disciplining that child as the child grows older than to begin or start disciplining a child suddenly when the child is "half grown" and not at all accustomed to being disciplined.

It's tough enough to discipline your own children. What if one or both of you have children from previous relationships? The brand new parent may have more difficulty disciplining a child or children that are not theirs; biologically speaking that is.

It may be very difficult for a child to accept being disciplined by someone who is not his or her biological parent. And to complicate matters even more, it may be difficult for the biological parent to see their new spouse disciplining their child.

These are things that must be worked out slowly, deliberately, and carefully. It's in everyone's best interest to work them out so that ultimately the child will benefit and progress. The child's needs are paramount in this area.

Questions to Ask Before Taking the Leap

1. How well do you know your fiancé's family?
2. Have you met his or her parents?
3. Do you have any type of relationship with them?
4. Do you live nearby, perhaps in the same town or a neighboring community?
5. Do you live within a few hours of them?
6. Do you live in the same time zone?
7. Do you live in the same country?
8. How about your fiancé's siblings and their families?
9. Do you know them and do you have a relationship with them?
10. Does your fiancé have any children?
11. Do they live together or do the children live apart from your fiancé?
12. Do you foresee having children in your marriage?
13. Would you want a large family or a small family?
14. What is your definition of a small family and a large family?
15. How soon would you want to start a family?
16. If you have children from previous relationship(s) how interested are you in having more children with your new spouse?
17. If your relationship produced a pregnancy and you already had as many children as you wanted, what would you want to do?

Notes, thoughts, ideas, questions and issues I want to discuss with my love...

Chapter Fifteen

In the Event of...

All she keeps inside isn't on the label.

– Fuel

$\mathcal{S}$keletons from the past – Skeletons aren't always what they seem. "Skeletons" can be anything from health issues that could be potentially passed on to your children, to financial problems, past divorces, relationships and indiscretions. Open up the dialogue before you get married to discuss any skeletons that may present themselves in your relationship. Things to consider:

* Trust your inner voice. If something doesn't feel right or you're uneasy with certain aspects of your relationship, it's probably for good reason.

* Get everything out on the table that you may be hiding, and if you're hiding something from your partner, ask yourself why. Do you think your fiancé won't understand or will leave you? What's driving you to hide things?

* Ask those who you trust what their feelings are about things you aren't sure of. Could it just be your own insecurities, or is something just not right.

* Some who counsel those getting married will say, "Look deep before you leap." Have you looked deep?

* Unfaithfulness – There are several ways to be unfaithful. Here are three types of affairs that can occur:

  * Emotional affair – This type of affair occurs in relationships where one or both partners are feeling emotionally unfulfilled. They look outside of the marriage for love and acceptance to fulfill a need. The relationship may or may not be sexual, but sex isn't the primary reason the affair begins.

◆ Sexual affair – This type of affair occurs when one or both partners aren't feeling sexually fulfilled. One partner may require more frequent sexual encounters than the other and they go outside the marriage to have that need filled. The partner having the affair may "justify" the affair because it is only sexual. They may rationalize that since there are no emotions attached it's really not that bad.

◆ Online affair – This type of affair may start out as harmless, but since it's perpetrated over the Internet, the cheater may feel like they're not actually cheating at all.

Although an affair may seem like the end of a relationship, with patience, forgiveness, love and understanding, it can be worked through and your relationship can become stronger in the process.

The main things to remember are:

◦ Don't assume your marriage is over or that your partner no longer wants or desires you.

◦ It's not always about sex. Look at your marriage and ask yourself if there is some type of void, or if your spouse is simply not a monogamous person.

◦ Communicate with your spouse and try to find out the "why" behind the affair.

◦ Once you know the "why," if there is an obvious answer, can it be fixed?

◦ Ask questions about the affair and decide if you can trust your spouse again in the future.

- Look to Chapter Twelve in the section on forgiveness. Can you truly forgive your partner?

- Abuse – Abuse comes in two forms: physical, and non-physical. Whether it's physical or not, abuse is still abuse. If your partner shows signs of abusive tendencies, you must know that if they don't seek counseling, the abuse may only get worse. Here are a few signs to look for that most abusers will show:

  - Jealousy – Oftentimes, the first sign you'll notice is jealousy. Abusers confuse jealousy with displaying love.

  - Control – Abusers want control over your every move. In the beginning, it will be something that may seem insignificant, but the need for control will grow as your relationship progresses.

  - Distorted Reality – Abusers will have a different view of what you should be other than who you actually are. They'll try to change you and mold you into their reality.

  - Fast to Commit – Abusers fall fast and hard and before you can catch your breath, you'll be in a committed relationship with them.

  - Cut Family Ties – Abusers don't want their prey to have close contacts with any friends or family. The severing of the ties will happen over time and you may not realize what's occurring, but your loved ones will wonder what happened to you and why you're not socially active like you once were. If you're ever confronted with that question, don't be in denial - stop and think.

  - Play the Blame Game – Abusers think that their behavior is because of what someone else did to them or because you're not doing what you're supposed to do to make them happy.

  - Striking the Walls – Just because someone hits a wall rather than you does not mean they won't strike you the next time.

If you suspect that you're in a relationship with an abuser, or your partner has any of the above tendencies, take a long hard look at your relationship and determine if you should get out while you're ahead.

Conversely, if you recognize any of these tendencies in yourself, seek counseling before you commit to marriage and weed out the source of your pain before you strike out against the one you love.

* Dependencies – There are several different types of dependencies that can affect your marriage. Here I list four, along with some helpful links to gain control and take back your life:

    1. Alcohol and chemical dependencies -http://usgovinfo.about.com/cs/healthmedical/a/drugabuse.htm

        * Alcohol – Information on alcoholic dependencies - http://www.alcoholics-anonymous.org/en_information_aa.cfm

        * Al-Anon can offer help to the family and friends of an alcoholic - http://www.al-anon.alateen.org/about.html

    2. Substance abuse – Prescription and non-prescription

        * About Prescription Drug addiction -http://www.prescriptiondrugaddiction.com/about.asp

        * Narc-Anon helps with drug addiction problems -http://www.drugsolutions.org/

        * Illegal substances and the motivation behind taking them - http://education.yahoo.com/reference/encyclopedia/entry/drugaddi

        * Effect of meth and illegal substances on the body -http://www.counselingseattle.com/drugs/meth.htm

        * Help for families and friends of crack addicts -http://groups.msn.com/SupportForFamilyFriendsOfCrackAddicts/

    3. Gambling Addiction - What is it and how can you get help? http://www.addictionrecov.org/addicgam.htm

        * Gambling addiction Q & A- http://www.addictionrecov.org/qandagam.htm

        * Signs, phases and treatment options -http://www.topcondition.com/images/mymindfield/gambling_addiction.htm

    4. Technology –

- Television - Not just a metaphor -http://www.sciam.com/print_version.cfm?articleID=0005339B-A694-1CC5-B4A8809EC588EEDF

- Identification and self-help guide -http://www.turnoffyourtv.com/healtheducation/addiction/addiction.html

- A growing problem- http://www.allaboutlifechallenges.org/television-addiction.htm

- Internet - "can be as destructive as alcoholism" http://library.albany.edu/briggs/addiction.html

- Center for online addiction -http://www.netaddiction.com/

- Can impact the workplace -http://www.addictionrecov.org/wrkguide_www.htm

- Pornographic materials - Accountability is essential -http://www.firesofdarkness.com/accountability.htm

- Sex addict or porn addict? How to tell... http://www.safe-families.org/amiaddicted.php

- How it impacts the family of the addict -http://www.azcentral.com/12news/news/articles/050206pornaddictwebpromo-CR.html

- Workaholics – Yes, this is a real problem...

  - Finding balance - http://www.allaboutlifechallenges.org/workaholic.htm

  - When enough really is enough... http://goliath.ecnext.com/comsite5/bin/pdinventory.pl?pdlanding=1&referid=2750&item_id=0199-1405364

  - Managing life with a workaholic -http://www.allaboutlifechallenges.org/living-with-a-workaholic-faq.htm

Questions to Ask Before Taking the Leap

1. Do you feel it's necessary and/or honest to discuss all of the skeletons in your respective closets or could that be potentially harmful?

2. If you or your fiancé/spouse did not want to discuss a skeleton in one or both of your closets, how would you feel?

3. If your fiancé/spouse confided in you about something in their past, would you look at them differently or judge them?

4. If your fiancé/spouse developed an addiction would you be able to support them in combating it?

5. Do you have an enabling personality?

6. How would you feel if an addiction you have hurt your fiancé/spouse or your family?

7. Would you stay with your spouse if they were ever abusive to you?

8. Do you have expectations on how you want to be treated by your fiancé/spouse?

9. Do you have clearly defined limits and boundaries that you would consider absolutely unacceptable if your fiancé/spouse crossed the line?

10. Have you shared these with your fiancé/spouse?

Notes, thoughts, ideas, questions and issues I want to discuss with my love...

Chapter Sixteen
Wills

Everybody wants to be somebody; nobody wants to grow.

– Johann Wolfgang von Goethe

$\mathcal{H}$ere's a morbid subject for a couple to discuss and consider…

Do you have a will?

Do you need a will?

Do you have children?

Do you have assets that you would want your loved ones to have instead of the state in the event of your untimely death?

These are very difficult questions for anyone to have to answer at any time. They are especially difficult questions for young people who feel that they're just beginning to live and have their whole lives ahead of them. But they are even more difficult due to the fact that you're preparing to get married.

However, it's a good idea to have a will, no matter your age or state of health. If you don't have a will and you die, the laws of the state in which you reside or a judge will decide who gets your property, assets and even your children. They are not likely to make the same choices and decisions that you would make. That is why a will is so important. If you wait too long, it could be too late.

In most cases, wills are mostly simple, straight forward documents that can be relatively inexpensive if prepared by an attorney. There are several resources that you can refer to that can even help you prepare a will on your own. However, if your situation is more complex, you'd probably be best served by hiring an attorney.

There are a few basic elements required to ensure your will is legal and covers all of the bases it should. At a minimum:

* Your will should list all of your most important assets and to whom you would like to leave each asset.

* It should name all of your children and dependents and name the person or people who you would like to raise them until they are of

the age of majority. The people you name should be informed and in agreement before you list them in your will.

* Your will should name those who would manage any property you leave to your children.

* Your will should be signed in front of witnesses.

* Your will should be stored in a safe place and one that the executor knows of the whereabouts.

Once you have a will, it should be updated as your family grows and as you acquire more assets.

Living Wills

Life is not governed by will or intention. Life is a question of nerves, and fibers, and slowly built-up cells in which thought hides itself and passion has its dreams.

– Oscar Wilde

You have the right to decide for yourself what medical decisions you would like to make on your own behalf in the event that you are severely injured or suffer a debilitating illness or health problem. For instance, if you are involved in an accident, or suffer from a health event that leaves you in a coma, by completing a living will, tough medical questions are "pre-answered" by you on your behalf. If it is your desire, in the event that you end up in a coma, to turn off any life supporting equipment, the living will is where you can declare your wishes.

Similarly, if you were to end up in a coma, and there were little chance that you could ever gain consciousness, would you want them to keep the life support machines operating indefinitely?

What if your medical prognosis was that even if you did regain consciousness, your quality of life would never resemble what it used to be? Would you still want a fighting chance by keeping yourself alive and dependent on life support equipment? This is your choice and it is expressed legally in a living will.

There have been numerous cases (some played out in the media), in which there has been an absence of a living will, and people have found themselves in this predicament. When that happens, usually it is the next of kin who has to make that decision for you. Their decision can be contested by other loved ones, and that is where it gets very, very emotional and complicated. I mean, it's already a horrible situation that you're in a coma. Having fights over your medical treatment just makes a horrible situation worse for everyone involved.

Your reasons for your decision may be religious based or based on your strong personal beliefs. You can have your wishes met and eliminate emotional and mental stress and trauma for many of those closest to you by completing a living will.

What if you're in an accident and you don't survive? Having a living will can enable you to donate one or more functioning body parts to a very needy recipient. If you choose to be a donor, this must be decided ahead of time and must be legally documented. Having this documentation on your driver's license may not be enough if your family or loved ones contest it.

A living will not only protects your last wishes, it also protects those who will make decisions on your behalf after you're gone. Guilt can be a powerful thing and if your loved ones doubt the decisions they've made for you, they could live with guilt for the rest of their lives. By creating a living will while you're of sound mind and body, you've relieved those you care about from making those types of decisions; they know what you would want them to do.

Questions to Ask Before Taking the Leap

1. Do you and/or your fiancé/spouse have any children?
2. Do you and/or your fiancé/spouse own property?
3. Do you and/or your fiancé/spouse own a business?
4. Do you and/or your fiancé/spouse have assets?
5. Do you and/or your fiancé/spouse have a will?
6. Do you have a power of attorney?

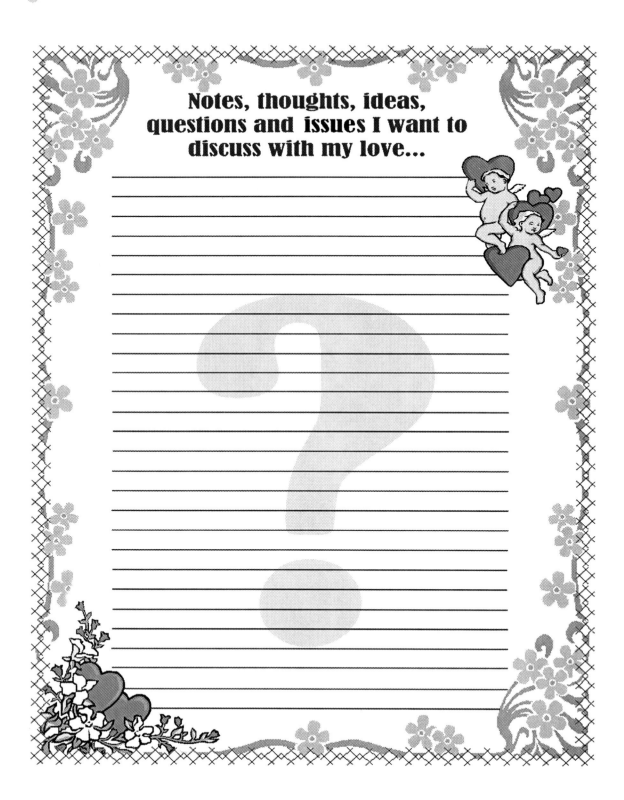

**Notes, thoughts, ideas,
questions and issues I want to
discuss with my love...**

Summary

Congratulations on purchasing and reading this book! You have made a very wise choice for your future. If this book was a gift, then thank the person who bought it for you (they truly care about you and your marriage!) and give yourself a pat on the back for reading it! Give a copy of this book to your fiancé or spouse, and support them in reading it too! Purchase a copy for everyone you know and love who shares with you their plans to get married! It's an extremely loving and caring gift.

I hope the information in this book helps you on your journey to a very successful, happy, and fulfilling marriage. Obviously, not all of the information I have provided will apply to every engaged or newlywed couple. However, some applies to each and every couple who marries, as they are solid, life lessons.

There are loads of ideas contained in this book. Some of them will apply to you directly. Others may or may not apply in the future. Re-read it in a few months to a year; you'll be surprised at how many changes you'll experience between now and then.

Take notes and talk things over with the love of your life. Make sure you are on track to developing the very best marriage you can imagine! Some of these good habits will come easily and naturally. Other good habits will take longer to establish, especially when bad habits have to first be broken. Keep working at it. It's worth it! When you think about it, you've already bet your life on it!

Put the ideas and concepts presented here into action. Reading about it and doing nothing won't do you any good. Remember -- the goal here is to establish the best possible marriage you can imagine. You're worth it!

Talk with your partner. Discuss the issues, tips, and advice scattered throughout this book. Also, perhaps something you read may trigger other thoughts you want to discuss with your fiancé or spouse that you had never thought would be an issue. If you read something in the book that is difficult to discuss, highlight it or circle it and ask your partner to read it. (Blame me!) That may "break the ice," allowing a discussion to take place afterward. Use the "Notes, thoughts, ideas, questions and issues I want to discuss with my love…" page at the end of each chapter to record anything else you think of that you'd like to communicate with your partner.

You are about to enter or have recently entered a beautiful marriage. That is so wonderful! CONGRATULATIONS! Get your marriage off to a great start! Develop wonderful, loving, generous habits now! It's so much easier to maintain the great habits you implement now, early in your relationship, instead of getting off to a rocky start and then a few years down the road having to put on the breaks and change course in order to save a troubled marriage. This, my friend, is the entire purpose of this book!

Drop me a line! If this book helped you in any way, I'd love to hear from you. Whether it was a large, enormously difficult topic that presented many challenges, or a simple thing that went overlooked, I'd be thrilled if you shared your story with me.

Contact me at www.kissthebridenowwhat.com

I wish you all the best in your marriage!

About the Author

If your ship hasn't come in, don't wait, go out there and get it!

– Reginald Wickham

*R*eginald Wickham was born on August 17, 1958 in Brooklyn, New York and raised in Teaneck, New Jersey. He received a Bachelor of Science degree in Electrical Engineering from the University of Bridgeport in May, 1980.

He worked as an Electrical Engineer immediately after graduation. Self-taught in the field of Computer Programming, he changed careers in 1984 and within five years of working in this new field he became an independent consultant working with numerous clients in various industries in the private sector as well as governmental and military organizations. Between his two professional careers, he has traveled to more than 30 states and has also worked in Toronto, Canada; Guadalajara, Mexico; and Madrid, Spain.

Currently, he resides in Gonzales, LA, a small town in Louisiana located between New Orleans and Baton Rouge with his new bride, Trudy Bell.

Wickham is quite accustomed to taking on new and challenging adventures. His list of past and present hobbies and accomplishments is mind boggling and includes, but is certainly not limited to:

Tennis, racquetball, golf, horseback riding and equestrian barrier jumping, white-water rafting, kayaking, canoeing, water skiing, downhill skiing, cross country skiing, hiking, mountain climbing and bicycling and he is an internationally certified SCUBA diver. In addition Wickham, who taught himself to play the bass guitar as a teenager, co-founded a group called, "N2N" (pronounced In Tune). N2N has enjoyed great success performing at weddings, parties and clubs from Baton Rouge to world-famous Bourbon St. in New Orleans.

More seriously, Wickham has served on the board of directors of three enterprises. Of all of his accomplishments he is most proud of his tenure with a not-for-profit organization.

This non-profit concern based in New York, NY was organized to raise monies used for tuition for private schools. This allowed African-American elementary school aged males who had been labeled "Special Education Students" to attend and excel in private schools. "The success rate of this program was phenomenal. Once these youths were in an environment where excellence was expected, mediocrity was not accepted and support and love were abundant; they thrived!" During the height of this program, Wickham, who served as Executive Vice President, personally paid for up to three full tuitions per year out of his own pocket. "Our organization has received letters from alumni saying that we have literally saved their lives. I consider that the ultimate compliment a service based organization can receive."

Wickham is a natural leader who wants to help others. As a consultant, he has had an opportunity to help numerous people in numerous companies all across our nation. On his own time he has participated as a tutor to many children and serves his community volunteering as a mentor and facilitator for various organizations.

It is this side of Wickham's persona that inspired and motivated him to write this book. Wickham saw a need and wrote this book to help couples engaging in a new marriage to build strong relationships based on honest communication. There is a plethora of books based on love. There are hundreds of books based on rebuilding marriages that are failing. This book was written to prevent marriages from suffering common, avoidable pitfalls by encouraging honest discussion on a variety of subject matters. It was also written to highlight common topics that many, if not most, newlyweds face – but seldom discuss. From very serious topics (like saving, investing and budgeting) to relatively light topics (like who's going to wash the dishes), these issues can cause tension, arguments and worse in a marriage. "If my book can help couples to enjoy a better relationship, then I am eternally thankful."

I welcome you to visit www.kissthebridenowwhat.com Share your stories on how better communication has contributed to your marriage and relationship. Tell me what information in this book truly resonated with you. Tell me your memorable episodes – whether good, bad, funny or otherwise noteworthy as it relates to the topics mentioned in this book!

Illustrations by Nancy Park

Nancy Park lives in Oklahoma with her husband and four cats. She has done commercial illustrations since 1965 -- from fashion to farm equipment to cartoons. Retired now, Nancy does commissioned oil portraits. Her website is www.NancyParkArt.com.

Front cover photography contributed by Phil Royal

Member Professional Photographer's of America (PPA)

PPA Certified

www.photobyphilroyal.com

Photograph of author by Reginald Wickham, Sr.

Reginald Wickham, Sr. has been acclaimed as a master photographer who uses a great deal of imagination to create striking photographic effects. Skillfully, he specializes in combining the techniques of photography, art, and lithography.

www.kissthebridenowwhat.com

[1] Wong, Grace. CNN Money.com. 20 May, 2005. 12 September, 2006. http://money.cnn.com/2005/05/20/pf/weddings/.

[2] Linda J. Waite and Maggie Gallagher, *The Case for Marriage: Why Married People are Happier, Healthier, and Better Off Financially*, (New York Doubleday, 2000), p. 64.

[3] Katherine Reissman and Naomi Gerstel, "Marital Dissolution and Health: Do Males or Females Have Greater Risk?" *Social Science and Medicine* 20 (1985): 627-635.

[4] James Q. Wilson, *The Marriage Problem: How Our Culture Has Weakened Families* (New York: Harper Collins, 2002), p. 16.

[5] Lois Verbrugge and Donald Balaban, "Patterns of Change, Disability and Well-Being," *Medical Care* 27 (1989): S128-S147.

[6] Robert Coombs, "Marital Status and Personal Well-Being: A Literature Review," *Family Relations* 40 (1991) 98.

[7] Linda J. Waite, "Does Marriage Matter?" *Presidential Address to the American Population Association of America*, April 8, 1995.

[8] Robert T. Michael, et al., *Sex in America: A Definitive Survey*, (Boston: Little, Brown, and Company, 1994), p. 124-129.

[9] U.S. Department of Justice, Office of Justice Programs, Bureau of Justice Statistics, (March 1994), p. 31, NCJ-145125.

[10] Richard Rogers, "Marriage, Sex, and Mortality," *Journal of Marriage and the Family* 57 (1995): 515-526.

[11] United States Department of Agriculture. (2005, January). *Dietary Guidelines for Americans, 2005*. Retrieved October 31, 2006, from http://www.health.gov/dietaryguidelines/dga2005/recommendations.htm.

Bonus! Free Compatibility Questionnaire!..

Are you contemplating marriage?
Are you engaged?
Are you a newlywed?

You May Kiss the Bride!
(Now What?)
The Essential Plan for the Marriage of Your Dreams

An incredibly valuable resource;
a comprehensive guide for planning your dream marriage!

Do you have a daughter, soon to be a bride? Do you have a son, soon to be a groom? Do you have a relative, friend or coworker who is engaged to be married? Tell them about this book – now! (Or better yet, purchase it for them as a gift!) They will always remember you as the one who gave them the gift that helped them achieve their dream marriage! (Or if you'd like, they can think of you as the one who gave them a toaster, tray tables or a towel set!)

But now, order your free compatibility questionnaire! It presents a variety of in-depth questions, scenarios and areas of discussion designed to help you understand your mate, yourself, and the dynamics of your relationship a little better.

For your free bonus compatibility questionnaire, visit: www.kissthebridenowwhat.com
-or-
Fill out and mail in the coupon below:

Send me a Free Compatibility Questionnaire!

Name: _____
Address: _____
Email: _____
Telephone: _____

Mail this coupon to:
The Wickford Group, LLC
7516 Bluebonnet Boulevard
Suite 204
Baton Rouge, LA 70810-1627

Printed in the United States
100691LV00001B/67-76/A

9 781600 373381